WW II . . .
A Navy Nurse Remembers

WW II . . .
A Navy Nurse Remembers

Elizabeth Kinzer O'Farrell
LT (NC) USN (RET)

CyPress
Publications

Tallahassee, Florida

Copyright © 2007 by Elizabeth Kinzer O'Farrell

Inquiries should be addressed to:
CyPress Publications
P.O. Box 2636
Tallahassee, Florida 32316-2636
http://cypress-starpublications.com
lraymond@nettally.com

Library of Congress Cataloging-in-Publication Data

O'Farrell, Elizabeth Kinzer, 1919-
   WW II- a navy nurse remembers / Elizabeth Kinzer O'Farrell. — 1st ed.
       p. cm.
    ISBN-13: 978-0-9776958-6-7 (pbk.)
    ISBN-10: 0-9776958-6-7 (pbk.)
   1. O'Farrell, Elizabeth Kinzer, 1919- 2. World War, 1939-1945—Medical care—United States. 3. World War, 1939-1945—Personal narratives, American. 4. United States. Navy—Nurses—Biography. 5. Nurses—United States—Biography. I. Title. II. Title: World War Two— a navy nurse remembers. III. Title: World War 2— a navy nurse remembers.

   D807.U6O42 2007
   940.54'7573092—dc22
   [B]

                                        2007032388

ISBN 13: 978-0-9776958-6-7
ISBN 10: 0-9776958-6-7

First Edition

Dedication

To my long-ago patients, wherever they may be,
and to the medical staff who worked
with me caring for them.

Acknowledgment

My thanks to my World War II
veteran husband John, and to his
son John III, for their interest in and
help that made this book possible.

Contents

Photographs

Photographs—Continued

Prologue

Four or five years ago during an informal (no assigned speaker) meeting of the Tallahassee, Florida, chapter of the World War II Historical Society, a member turned to me and suggested I tell the members about my experiences as a Navy nurse during World War II. Startled, I didn't know what to say. I had never left the country during the war. I had never served overseas or aboard a hospital ship, but I had cared for many terribly hurt and disabled young men who had. Could I talk about them? Should I? I didn't know.

With the society members waiting for me to say something—anything—I finally said, "But . . . but nobody was shooting at me! I was still in nursing school in 1941 when the Japanese bombed Pearl Harbor, and the war in Europe was winding down when I graduated and got my nursing license (RN) in 1943."

While I only occasionally attended meetings of the World War II Historical Society with my veteran husband, a survivor of "The Battle of the Bulge," I had never thought of myself as a member of the society, nor that my service during the war deserved historical mention. I knew I had been doing a job I really cared about and was well prepared to do, but I hadn't really gone to war or experienced it as most of the members of the society described it. Nevertheless, after the meeting I consented to be interviewed, to tell my stories

1

about my experiences during the war as I lived them from December 7, 1941, until July 1950 when I resigned my commission as a lieutenant in the Navy Nurse Corps to go back to school and resume a civilian life.

During the next several years, my husband and I were invited to talk about our experiences during World War II in a number of high school history classes and memorial events around Tallahassee. Because I had worked previously as an editor for a nursing journal, a friend suggested I write about my experiences in the war for publication. A challenge? Perhaps, but my stories are all about working with patients I shall never forget, and I hope you, the reader, will see and understand why my experiences working with my patients during World War II was the high point in my nursing career.

Japan Attacks Pearl Harbor

I was a senior nursing student at The Presbyterian Hospital School of Nursing in Chicago when the Japanese attacked Pearl Harbor on December 7, 1941. On that now so-called "infamous" Sunday morning I was on duty on the men's medical-surgical floor of the hospital. Sundays in those days were usually uneventful, a quiet time on the wards with patients resting, reading (usually the *Chicago Daily Tribune*), listening to their radio or, if able, visiting with other patients on the ward while they waited for lunch and visiting hours.

As I went hurriedly about my duties completing the patients' morning care before lunch trays arrived, I began to hear patients talking about something catastrophic happening in Hawaii and that President Roosevelt was going to be making an important announcement about it on the radio that afternoon. No one seemed to know what had happened. Finally, an excited ambulatory patient who had been listening to the radio in the sunroom came in to tell us that the Japanese had bombed the U.S. Naval Base at Pearl Harbor.

As a student nurse, I wasn't up on politics or on much of anything else relative to the war in Europe, but I did wonder. Why would the Japanese bomb Pearl Harbor? More important, I wondered what all this might mean to the class of '42. I was to find out that afternoon when I joined other members of our class to listen to the President on the radio in the nurses' quarters telling us that the Japanese had attacked our fleet in Pearl Harbor without warning and that he had asked Congress for a declaration of war against Japan.

The year 1942 soon became an anxious time for the class of '42. We had much to worry about that spring and summer; graduation, the State Board Examination for our nursing license, and decisions about the future lay ahead. News about the war on both European and Pacific fronts generated additional and sometimes personal concern via news from home about a family member, a close friend, or a sweetheart going off to war.

The what-to-do after graduation became a favorite off-duty topic for us. Some in our class said they planned to join the Army Nurse Corps right after graduation. Others opted for the Navy Nurse Corps. Some said they planned to stay on as a staff nurse at the hospital. Still others, whose sweethearts were already in the service or soon would be, decided to go home and get married right after graduation.

The what-to-do-after-graduation decision was not a difficult decision for me to make. I grew up and went to school in a rural community ninety miles southwest of Chicago where the most exciting activity during an entire summer might be the Sunday School picnic at Starved Rock State Park. According to my mother, even while I was a little kid the grass was always a little greener for me someplace else, and I decided if I was to see some of the someplace(s) else I so wanted to see, the Navy Nurse Corps was probably the right decision for me.

October 26, 1942, it was official. I had graduated from the School of Nursing. I had passed the State Board Examination and gotten my license to practice nursing, and I had decided to join the Navy. After a brief holiday at home to visit my family, to catch up on the war news there, and to tell them that I had decided to join the Navy, I sent in

4

my application for a commission in the United States Navy Nurse Corps. Then I hired on as a temporary staff nurse at the hospital and settled down to wait for orders.

Days became weeks, and the weeks became months without any word from the Navy. Finally an official looking letter arrived for me from Washington DC, dated 17 May 1943. The message was a surprise but perfectly clear. I was ". . . to make an appointment to have a physical examination by a Naval Medical Officer at the Naval Training Center, Navy Pier, Chicago, Illinois." I was not happy. Had I known how the system worked, I might have been, but I thought I was to be stationed at the medical dispensary at Navy Pier, Chicago, Illinois. Fortunately, lesson one on waiting for orders cleared up that misconception. After my physical examination, the medical officer at the Naval Training Center informed me that I was to go home and wait until I heard from the Bureau of Medicine and Surgery in Washington. On July 6th I received a brief message from that august body:

```
Elizabeth Emma Kinzer of Chicago, Illinois
is hereby appointed a reserve nurse in
the Navy Nurse Corps, to serve whenever
needed, to _____, _____, . . .
```

The whenever and wherever were nowhere mentioned.

The next letter, this one from the Bureau of Naval Personnel and dated 7 August 1943, made my call to duty official.

```
Subject: Orders:

1. You are hereby called to active duty.

2. On or about 31 August, you will proceed
to Great Lakes, Illinois and report to the
```

August 31, 1943, U.S. Naval Hospital, Great Lakes, Illinois

The grass at the Great Lakes Naval Hospital was not a whole lot greener than anywhere else I had ever been, but my nursing career was the beginning of a whole new way of life for me. The first big change was the Navy nurse's dress uniform with its severely tailored, double-breasted black suit worn with a long-sleeved, buttoned-collar-and-cuffs white shirt and black tie, matronly black shoes and stockings, and all this topped off by a round, flat, white hat with the American Eagle perched grandly on a black headband that sat squarely on the wearer's brow. Fortunately, the Navy nurse's dress uniform has become far less masculine, and undoubtedly far more comfortable as well, since World War II. Our duty uniforms were more user-friendly and not too different from those we wore as civilians, except for the heavily starched box-like nurse's cap with a black velvet band to which a single or double gold braid was attached, depending on the wearer's military rank. White hose and shoes were essentially like those worn by civilian nurses.

Another change that took even more getting used to was the military drills we were expected to participate in. I had no problem telling my right foot from my left one, but I never really mastered the art of marching in formation. I was not alone. Our often frustrated drill master soon gave up yelling at us, probably because it didn't seem to help. We simply were not soldiering material.

Actual nursing practice at Great Lakes was the greatest change for me and required a whole new point of view. I was stationed at the Great Lakes Naval Hospital for six months without caring for more than a half dozen patients who actually needed professional nursing care—a not particularly remarkable situation of course since most of our patients there at that time were healthy young men and more often than not new recruits.

My first duty assignment was to a multiple-bed, ear-nose-and-throat, barracks-type ward where the most common malady was referred to by both doctors and patients alike as "cat-fever." I soon learned that cat-fever had nothing to do with cats. It was short for catarral inflammation, a malady better known as the common cold. The terms "cat-fever" and "catarral inflammation," of course, are not actual medical terms as such, but common usage made them popular as a quick and easy diagnosis for an otherwise healthy young man with a bad cold or sniffles. I soon learned, too, that entry nursing for the Navy Nurse Corps, for good reason was primarily a matter of teaching and supervising the training of corpsmen in the basic principles of patient care, personal hygiene, and health maintenance skills they would need when on sea duty or in actual combat situations.

Recreation opportunities were not exactly plentiful at Great Lakes, probably because the base is situated equidistance by train from Chicago and Milwaukee, Wisconsin, cities known by Navy personnel at the time as "good liberty" towns. Although there were tennis courts, a bowling alley, the Officers Club, and a boathouse available to us, our recreation time for the most part was spent getting together in one room or the other in the nurses' quarters to swap stories, share news of the war, and goodies sent from home.

I did, however, have one short session trying my hand at sailing.

My roommate, a classmate and graduate from The Presbyterian Hospital School of Nursing who got her orders to Great Lakes three months before I got mine, was invited to take sailing lessons by one of the cadets at the boathouse. This seemed a great idea, and I signed on for the lessons, too. Ann's sailing instructor taught her to sail. They were married less than a year later and were still married and still sailing for many years after the war was over. My instructor, however, liked to do all of the sailing. I was just along for the ride. Either he thought I was too inept to be a student worthy of his attention, or he thought I would be happy just watching him do the sailing. In any event, when he ran the boat aground and I laughed, he suggested I would never be a good sailor, and I agreed not to come back for any more lessons.

Winter came and went. So did many nurses. My roommate, Ann, who liked the top bunk, got her orders for the medical dispensary in Quantico, Virginia. Barbara, a new nurse fresh from civilian life, moved in. Barbara wanted the bottom bunk. I agreed to switch to the top bunk, and life went on. The corpsmen on my ward did most of the nursing care. I made rounds with the doctor, did the routine paper work, and hoped I would soon get orders to someplace else. That problem was solved on March 20th. I got the following orders:

> . . . On or about 30 March 1944 you will regard yourself detached from the Naval Hospital, Great Lakes . . . Will proceed to Glenview, Illinois, and report to Commanding Officer Naval Air Station for duty at Naval Dispensary.

Glenview Naval Air Station: 30 March 1944–24 April 1945

Glenview, Illinois, was thirty miles closer by bus to Chicago than Great Lakes, and the grass was no greener there than anywhere else I had ever been. But no matter; since I knew almost nothing about airplanes and had never been on one, I thought it might be fascinating to meet some of the men who flew them. That part was correct, but nursing duty at Glenview was even less demanding than it had been at Great Lakes.

I was one of six nurses stationed at the dispensary, and again our duties involved teaching and supervising medical corpsmen. Our patients, however, were very different. Glenview Naval Air Station in 1944 was a training base for Navy and Marine pilots, many of whom were instructors for cadets fresh out of officer training schools, and others who were accomplished pilots training in advanced fighter aircraft for sea duty. In addition, there were the line officers and staff in command, a medical officer, a maintenance crew for the aircraft, and the usual supportive naval personnel at dispensary, flight line, mess hall, grounds, etc.

The nurses, because we were commissioned officers and there were only six of us, were housed on the base in the Bachelor Officers Quarters, commonly referred to as the BOQ. We had four rooms with connecting bath between rooms, and shared the dining room, the lounge, the bar, and game rooms with the other officers.

Sounds ideal? In many ways it was, but the mood on the base was as serious as its ultimate objective. These beautiful young men were going to war. They were being prepared to handle sophisticated military aircraft at sea, to take off and land on an aircraft carrier underway in an unfriendly sea. Duty at Glenview was serious business for these very special young men, and to me they became very special indeed.

Most of the patients we saw in the dispensary had only minor cuts and bruises—a sprain, a broken nose with black eyes, usually compliments of a bar brawl while on liberty but sometimes the result of a sloppy landing on a training flight. And of course there were the usual and ever popular cases of cat-fever, for which the well established treatment was a couple of APC's (aspirin, phenacitin, and caffeine) followed by a good night's sleep, then back to duty in the morning. Unfortunately, we also had our fair share among both officers and enlisted men who had acquired an STD (sexually transmitted disease) during a careless sexual encounter. Such patients were on house detention and were required to report to the dispensary each morning for their penicillin shot. It was a difficult time for these patients for two reasons: 1. If they were either officer or cadet, they were grounded until tested cured; and 2. They suffered from a leper-like syndrome among their fellows. The medical officer usually gave the penicillin shots along with a lecture, but we occasionally gave the shot and spared them the lecture.

Even as a student nurse I hated being on night duty. With only six nurses on the base, my turn for night duty came up far more often than I liked. Most nights we had no more than one or two patients on sick call, and the wee hours before dawn were always dreadful. After a while, to stay awake, I would wander just outside the admitting room to talk with whoever might still be up and around. Sometimes I shared a cup of coffee with a tipsy sailor coming in from liberty or a lonely, up-tight cadet coming up from the flight line. Sometimes I would just sit and talk with the night corpsman on duty about his life back in Mississippi, or I would ask him to cover for me while I went for a walk down to the flight line to watch the touch-and-go night flight training sessions. Staying awake, avoiding getting caught taking a five- or ten-minute nap on duty, was a major problem for me. Even though many nights there were no patients in sick bay, we were on standby duty in case of emergency at the flight line or a visit from the MPs (Military Police) with one or a half dozen beat-up sailors in tow.

Actually, looking back on night duty at Glenview, it was often a more rewarding time for me than day duty. People who work night shifts tend to philosophize, to think and reason about things important to them, to talk with others about things they don't understand or that frighten them— like going off to war and maybe getting killed, and I began even then to understand that a good listener is more than half-way toward becoming a truly sensitive, caring human being and a good nurse.

About recreation at Glenview, it was far more interesting than it had been at Great Lakes. We were young, reasonably attractive, and single. (Navy nurses during World War II were to remain single or be summarily discharged.) More to the point, of course, we lived in the BOQ. We dined in the Officers Mess with the other officers. We also used the game room, lounge, and bar if we elected to do so. We did not abuse these privileges, and in turn, we were never abused or harassed by the men we met who used them. For example, and there were many such, a Marine officer on temporary duty checking out in a Corsair, the fighter aircraft with gull-like wings popular during WWII, invited me to join him for a drink in the bar after dinner one evening. It was a pleasant evening, and several other officers joined us at the bar. My companion introduced me to a delightful drink called "Tom Rose," taught me how to play liars' dice, warned me not to play it with a drunken sailor, then accepted a challenge from the other officers present to teach me to play pool. He left the base a few days later. I never saw him again. I don't even remember his name these many years later, but I never play pool without remembering that fine Marine and his excellent advice, ". . . always when you play pool, Elizabeth, be sure you play with someone you know, and please, please, be careful not to dig up the felt on the pool table with your pool cue."

Did he survive the war? I sometimes wonder, but so many fine young men and officers came and went at Glenview during 1944 that their names and faces have become blurred in my memory.

One other adventure for me at Glenview relative to recreation deserves mention here. Although it would properly have been frowned on at the time had the commanding officer learned about it, I got my first flight one quiet Sunday afternoon in a B-25 bomber. The flight instructor smuggled me aboard along with the crew, and I watched right along with the cadets when the bomb bay doors were opened in flight. Of course, no bombs were aboard on a training flight, but I was glad enough after looking down through the open bomb bay doors at the potential target to go back to and remain in my bucket seat for the rest of the flight.

D-Day, June 6, 1944, was a turning point not just for the war in Europe, but for us at Glenview as well. Life became hectic with the increased coming and going of flight training personnel. Night duty at the dispensary got busier, with ambulances screaming up from the flight line with cadets pushed too hard to solo too soon by instructors too tired to do anything about it but pray. Working the night shift and trying to sleep during the day was hopeless. The graceful Corsair, which I loved to watch taking off if I was working days, was a disaster if I was working nights. Its powerful engine literally rattled the windows as it took off over the BOQ where I was trying to sleep. By fall I was getting tired, but everybody else on the base was getting tired too. Recreation had degenerated into huddling in room or lounge listening to war news, which was grim on both fronts. By Christmas that year, I was beginning to wonder, would I ever get to see someplace further than a hundred fifty miles in any direction from Chicago?

The year 1945 was to be a turnaround year in my Navy career. On February 19 the commanding officer at Glenview Naval Air Station received notice that I had completed a correspondence course in Navy Regulations and Customs with a mark of 3.89. Nobody could have been more surprised than I was. I suppose I knew I had taken the course at Great Lakes, because we were expected to take it, much as we were expected to participate in the military drills there, but a mark of 3.89 suggested I knew all about Navy Regulations and Customs, which could not have been further from the truth. That bit of news was followed almost immediately with a notice of my promotion to Lieutenant, Junior Grade. Now this was indeed good news. A Lt(jg) makes a better salary than an Ensign, but that was only part of the good news. I was due leave in March, and I had already made up my mind to take a trip to that someplace else I wanted so badly to see. If the Navy couldn't give me orders that would let me see something more of the world than I had seen so far, then I would simply take a trip on my leave to someplace I had never been.

Deciding where to go was easy. Ann, my classmate in nursing school and my first roommate at Great Lakes, had married her handsome sailing instructor, gotten her discharge from the Navy, and followed him to his new duty station in San Diego where she settled down to become a full-time wife and expectant mother. Ann wrote that she would be glad to have me come for a visit, and on March 15, with my round-trip ticket in hand, I climbed on a train in LaSalle Street Station, Chicago, heading west.

It was a great trip, which I shall not dwell on here because my story is not so much a travel log as a description of my life in the United States Navy Nurse Corps during World War II. Some comments taken from my trip log, however, do seem relevant to the transportation available at the time, to the people traveling, and to my reaction to them.

A natural question, perhaps, if asked today is, "Why take a train rather than a plane?" In 1945, there were few passengers and even fewer seats available on planes for passengers unless they were high-ranking officers or politicians traveling on war business. Besides being unavailable to low-ranking officers and enlisted personnel, space even on trains during WWII was not easy to come by. Military personnel traveling on orders had priority, and I knew I was fortunate to have gotten a seat on the train when it left LaSalle Street Station.

From My Trip Log:

March 16: Kansas City looks very much like Chicago. I missed crossing the Mississippi River. The porter said we crossed it at 2400. I must have dozed off. The train is jammed with soldiers and sailors, with more getting on at every stop. I've had to stay in my seat whenever we stop just in case more military personnel get on. If they are traveling on orders, I could get bumped. Really enjoyed going to the dining car for dinner on the train in between stops.

Trip Log:

March 17: Saturday, and we are in the desert. I had not nearly imagined what the desert would be like. The desolation is incredible. I would like to come back someday to see how anyone can live here. Seeing the mountains as we got closer to them was fascinating. There is some snow still on the crest of the tallest one. It looks much like the picture in the travel brochure, but I'm really tired of just sitting looking out the window. It might be fun to go see what all these soldiers and sailors are doing in the club car. Most of them are probably standing around drinking beer and swapping war news or stories about some horrific experience in boot camp. Others, especially the sailors, are likely to be huddled in a corner somewhere out of sight of the MPs, shooting craps. That is how it was at Great Lakes. When things got too quiet on the ward and there was much traffic back and forth to the head (the restroom aboard ship), I knew a crap game was in progress and that it was time to send in a corpsman to break it up. Haven't seen many women on the train, but maybe I'll get lucky and find someone to talk to in the club car.

Trip Log:

March 19: Had fun talking with a couple of sailors on their way to San Diego. They expect to be "shipping out" (getting sea duty) soon. Guess from the way they were talking, they really want to get into the war, to do something different and maybe really important before they settle down to some job back home after the war. The twenty-minute stopover in Tucson, Arizona, was fun. Indians there were selling silver and turquoise jewelry. I can't wear jewelry in uniform, of course, but I bought some turquoise earrings just for fun. Tucson, from the little I could see from the station, is a very different kind of city. I think I'd like to come back here someday. (I did in 1972, and I was right, Tucson was a different kind of city then.)

The next stop we made was in Tijuana, Mexico, I don't know why. But I enjoyed the few minutes I had trying to talk with the little kids begging pennies alongside the train. The next stop we will be in San Diego. I'll be glad to get there.

My trip log entries stopped abruptly when we arrived in San Diego, but I am sure I did all the touristy things any tourist would do, like visit the splendid zoo there and have lunch at the Coronado Hotel, a not easy thing to do in 1945 with admirals, rear admirals, captains, and other high-ranking Navy officers all over the place. My bright and shiny, new and "unsalty" (dulled by sea water and air) gold stripe and a half, indicating my rank as Lt(jg), made me feel definitely out of place there. But no matter; I was on leave, and I saw more gold braid in one brief lunch hour at the Coronado Hotel in San Diego than I saw gathered in one place the rest of WWII.

About San Diego, the city and the war, the city was virtually bursting at the seams with Navy personnel. Housing for young married officers and their wives was difficult to almost impossible to obtain. For enlisted men, it was whom they knew or just plain luck. Ann and her husband considered themselves luckier than many of the young married officers. They had a small apartment not far from the Navy base. They also had a comfortable couch, a car, and a single officer friend who helped them squire me around town.

It was an interesting trip and fun time for me in San Diego, but when it was time for me to leave I was glad enough to get on the train for the return trip to Chicago and my duty station in Glenview. Little did I anticipate it at the time, but my trip west had merely been the first leg of a cross-country trip to someplace else. I had barely settled back on duty at the dispensary when the commanding officer delivered the following orders for me:

```
   . . . Upon the reporting of your relief,
you will regard yourself detached from duty
at the Naval Dispensary, Naval Air Station,
Glenview, Ill., and from such other duty that
may have been assigned you; will proceed to
```

St. Albans Naval Hospital, NY: 7 May 1945–5 January 1946

Duty at St. Albans for me was an introduction to and beginning awareness of the reality of the war and the consequences for those who survived it. I was assigned duty on a post-trauma, surgical rehabilitation ward, where most of the patients were men who had sustained severe injuries and endured great trauma to both mind and body while in battle. For all practical purposes, the war was over for them, but the fight for survival was only just beginning. They were back home in the United States. They were sleeping on clean sheets in a hospital close enough to home for family and friends to come visit them. They had served their country, but they had no future. What was going to happen to them? How could they go home, hold a job, get married, raise a family? These were very real questions for which there were only terrifying or no satisfactory answers at all for them. How does one care for such patients? TLC, the acronym for tender loving care frequently applied to nursing care, is a simple answer, but these patients were not old men with some debilitating or life-threatening disease for which there may or may not be a cure. They were young men in their prime whose lives had been shattered by war.

I shall admit here that I did not know then how to help the patients on my ward beyond the TLC, which of course is indeed both basic and important to good nursing care. During the next four or five months, however, I began to understand. A man who has suffered and survived grievous injury at war feels alone. His companions, his "buddies" who shared his experiences under fire—a foxhole, a cigarette, a joke, maybe even a letter from home—are out there somewhere fighting and dying, and he feels left behind, frightened and terribly alone. He tries to remember what happened. Did his teammates make it? Did they go on without him, maybe thinking he was dead? Nights were the worst times for such patients, and I learned I could help them best by getting them to talk about their buddies, then letting them do so. It did not usually matter what they talked about. Sooner or later, with a few encouraging questions here and there, the story, with its fears and anxieties, would pour out. I never willingly discussed their injuries or what the future might hold for them because I knew in most cases that they would eventually be discharged either to their homes, if able, or to a veterans hospital for further treatment as needed to make room for the new patients arriving daily from field hospitals and hospital ships.

Even now, after sixty plus years, I still remember some of the patients on my ward at St. Albans Naval Hospital and wonder what happened to them. One such patient was John C. I shall call him by his first name only here because I have no wish to intrude on his privacy if by some chance he is still alive.

John C. was a Marine lieutenant who served somewhere in the South Pacific. He had suffered a sniper's bullet that damaged his spinal cord and left him totally paralyzed from the waist down. He had also sustained a bullet wound in his left shoulder that rendered his left arm more or less disabled as well. John had survived these terrible wounds, but very nearly did not survive the long and torturous trips from one field hospital to another before finally being flown into San

Francisco and thence to St. Albans so that he might receive care in a hospital close to his home.

When I first saw John C. I was shocked. He was terribly emaciated, unshaven, lost in a haze that I later learned was drug induced. Because of his extensive wounds, John had been kept as comfortable as possible on pain medication, on ample doses of morphine every four hours p.r.n. (as needed for pain). I had never before dealt with drug addiction, either inside or outside the hospital environment, but somehow I knew if this man was to live, we must get some nourishing food into him, get some control over his drug dependency, and if possible, restore his will to live. Fortunately, I did not know then how difficult that might be, and I lost the first round. John pushed the bowl of soup I was trying to feed him off the tray, onto the floor, and angrily demanded a shot for his pain. When I next suggested that the corpsman would be glad to give him a shave because his parents were coming and were anxious to see him, he refused to see them and demanded another shot for his pain.

This routine went on for several days. Finally, his mother, in tears, asked if they should just not try to see John for a while, and I realized then that the TLC approach was not the way to go with this patient. I told his parents not to give up on him and to come back the next day.

John's pain was real, but his parents' pain was also real. This wreck of a man was their son. He needed them, perhaps even more than they needed him, and I decided to try another approach. The next day I marched into John's room (he was in a private room because he was deemed critically ill) with a basin of hot water, some extra towels, shaving soap and a razor, and announced that if he wouldn't let the corpsman shave him, then I was going to do it. And I did. While I was at it, I gave him a bath, made up his bed fresh, and informed him that his parents would be coming in to see him during visiting hours. After that I gave him

21

his standing order medication for pain and promised him I would give him another if he needed it as soon as he had eaten all of his lunch so that he could be pleasant to and for his mother and father when they arrived.

While my new authoritative, pull-rank type approach in caring for John C. allowed me to win the first round in the fight for his survival, our fight was far from over. The battle with his drug dependency was a fierce one. It also was a valuable lesson for me. My authoritative, pull-rank approach to that problem of course did not work, and we were forced to resort to the usual procedure in treating a drug dependency case, e.g., every other dose of the addictive medication requested for pain relief would be a placebo, a harmless saline solution in the usual syringe in place of the drug. This did not always work, of course, because John's pain indeed was real, but it worked often enough and long enough between doses to gradually decrease the dosage while continuing to restore John's health and interest in living.

Eventually I was assigned to another ward to replace a nurse being transferred to a new assignment. I lost track of John after that and did not see him again until shortly before I was to be transferred to the Baruch Center of Physical Therapy at the Medical College of Virginia in Richmond. John had gained weight, was off the morphine, and looked great. I was glad to see him looking so much better, and for the opportunity to tell him so. I was also glad to see his smile and to know he not only recognized me, but seemed genuinely glad to see me. I still wonder sometimes about John C. and how he handled his handicap. I knew his chance of regaining much or any use of his lower back, hips, and legs was highly improbable.

But before telling you about my back-to-school experiences in Richmond, Virginia, perhaps I should mention that my tour of duty at the St. Albans Hospital was not an all-work-and-no-play assignment. I loved New York and became a frequent passenger on the special bus from the hospital into New York City on my days off. I soon learned how to get around the city on the subway, had a horse-drawn carriage ride in Central Park, went window shopping on Fifth Avenue, and visited St. Patrick's Cathedral, Saks Fifth Avenue, and Rockefeller Center across the street. One day I even took the ferry out to Ellis Island and the Statue of Liberty. That day was a clear, sparkling day, and I talked the guard on duty, who was not supposed to allow visitors to go inside the statue or to climb the stairs to the top (A safety measure not necessarily for the sake of the would-be visitor and climber but for the sake of the statue. Our country was at war.), into letting me make the climb. I am sure he thought I would get discouraged long before I reached the top. He was almost right, but it was thrilling indeed to reach that famous lady's crown and to stand looking out the windows in her crown at the incredible view of the cities and sea that surround her.

On V-J Day, August 15, 1945, a friend and I joined a wonderfully raucous, wildly celebrating crowd in Times Square. We missed the still famous kiss the media caught on film that day, but my date—a native New Yorker and a recovering patient on my ward—was inclined toward watching the celebration from the sidelines rather than becoming part of the crowd. He had only recently recovered his sight after having been temporarily blinded by an exploding bomb while on sea duty somewhere off the coast of England. I could understand his caution and was content enough to watch from the sidelines right along with him. My reward? Dinner in the Rainbow Room atop the RCA Building in Rockefeller Center.

One other episode in my New York adventures while stationed at St. Albans that can now be told these many years later was educational and fun. It bordered, however, on the brink of insubordination to a superior officer, a commodore, no less, on a submarine tender. Shortly before I was to leave St. Albans for my new assignment in Richmond, a patient on my ward about to be discharged after minor surgery back to his command aboard the U.S.S. Diablo (a submarine tied up on the Jersey shore for repairs) invited me to have dinner with him aboard the submarine. We were allowed to go into the city in civilian clothes then, but a visit by a naval officer aboard a commissioned naval vessel required military attire, and I had dressed appropriately for the occasion. "Skip" (not his real name) was popular with his crew, and he was enthusiastically welcomed back aboard by the crew on watch. Dinner was fun, with a few drinks and much laughter over a few sea stories probably cleaned up a bit for my benefit. After dinner Skip suggested we join some of his fellow officers at a makeshift officers club on the Jersey shore. There we had a few more drinks with Skip's fellow officers and friends, sang crazy songs like "Mairzy Doats" and "Chickery-Chick," and had a really good time. Then the commodore, who obviously had a head start at the bar, got pretty drunk, and Skip decided it was his responsibility to see that the commodore, a fellow officer, got safely back to his ship.

It was still early and the commodore insisted we join him for supper on the submarine tender (the so-called "mother hen" among naval vessels at sea whose duty and responsibility it is to tend her "chicks," the submarines in her fleet). That seemed like fun, and Skip and the seamen waiting to take the commodore out to his ship helped the inebriated commodore and this land lubber into the skiff that was waiting to take us out to the tender. Naturally, the seaman on watch piped us all aboard, and I was thrilled to return his salute. But the evening did not end there. We had a lovely supper elegantly prepared and served by the commodore's aide. Meanwhile, Skip was watching the time. The last ferry back to Manhattan and the bus that would take us back to St. Albans left promptly at 2300 hours. It had been a long time since I had seen a head (a restroom). I had also had more than usual for me to drink, and it was a long way back to St. Albans and the nurses' quarters. What to do? Finally, I asked and was offered use of the head in the commodore's quarters. His aide showed me the way and carefully closed the door behind me. Naturally, I looked around, and there neatly laid out on the turned down bed were the commodore's pajamas. The temptation won. I tied a knot in the legs of his pajamas, did what I came in to do, and rejoined our host in the mess. Skip knew I had been up to something and suggested we really had to catch the ferry if we were to get back to the base on time. We did catch the ferry, and of course, I did confess my momentary madness to Skip. He clucked a bit after we both stopped laughing, but it had been fun, and somehow I didn't really feel very guilty. Why would a salty old commodore who had spent a good portion of his life at sea need to have his bed turned down and his pajamas laid out for him?

A few days later Skip went back to the U.S.S. Diablo, and I went off to school in Richmond, Virginia. Looking back now at New York City then, it was a teeming, crowded, exciting, and happy place to visit. I had roamed the city visiting museums, parks, and churches, sometimes with friends, often alone, and I was never afraid. Sixty-plus years later, it is still teeming, still crowded, still exciting, but certainly no longer as safe or as happy a place to visit as it was for me in 1945.

Medical College of Virginia:
4 February 1946–18 August 1946

I arrived at the Medical College of Virginia along with seventeen other Navy nurses taking an accelerated course in Physical Therapy as ordered by the Bureau of Naval Personnel. We had learned earlier that housing arrangements would be made for us on arrival, that we would be living in private homes in the area, and that we would be expected to make our own arrangements about living expenses— food, laundry, transportation, etc., on a per diem basis. The Physical Therapy course at the Baruch Center would last six months and be followed immediately by a six-month apprenticeship program at a Naval hospital under the supervision of a physiatrist, a physician who specialized in the branch of medicine dealing with Physical Therapy.

Why Navy nurses for this program? After the "shooting war" ended (V-J Day, August 15, 1945, formal surrender was signed by the Japanese September 2), military personnel began leaving the service in large numbers based on a point system. Professional physical therapists served in the Navy as WAVES (Women Appointed for Voluntary Emergency Service) and were among those eligible to leave the service on the point system. Who better, with a crash training course, to take on the rehabilitation needs of patients arriving daily from hospital ships and field hospitals overseas than nurses interested in remaining in the Navy? To make the training program more attractive to such nurses, the proverbial "carrot on a stick" approach promised not just career enhancement for us, but college credit toward a Bachelor of Science degree as well. I had been disappointed while still at St. Albans when my orders for sea duty aboard a hospital ship were canceled, and I signed up for the course with a view toward getting my Bachelor of Science degree while still in the Navy. My application was accepted shortly after V-J Day. On October 2, 1945, I signed over from the U.S. Naval Reserve (USNR) to the regular Navy (USN) and was detached from the St. Albans Naval Hospital on January 25, 1946.

Getting the housing matter settled on arrival in Richmond, of course, was a priority, and since private accommodations were not made available to us, roommate selection was done by the count-off system. My roommate by this method turned out to be Josie, a nurse whom I shall call only by her first name here. Josie and I gathered our hand luggage, drew our housing address assignment from the list of homes available to us, and took a cab to the address we drew. I was somewhat apprehensive about all this until I saw the beautiful old house with a formal, well-tended garden that I would call home for the next six months.

Our host and hostess in Richmond were a middle-age southern lady and her husband whose grown children were off somewhere, the daughter at "finishing school," the son off somewhere else—in the service perhaps and not expected to come home while we were there. Josie and I occupied his room, which Mrs. Chappie (not her real name) had refurnished with twin beds, a desk, and an extra bedside lamp. Our bath was nearby in the hall and reserved for our use exclusively while we were there.

Since we were involved in an accelerated course at the Medical College, classes started the very next day. At first we took all our meals in the staff cafeteria at the college but soon found that tiresome for all three meals. Transportation and laundry were also a problem at first, but Mrs. Chappie helped with these problems. She had her husband bring us a detailed map of the city showing bus routes, shopping areas downtown, and a list of restaurants serving family-type meals.

About classes, back-to-school adjustment, and problems with hitting the books again, I shall be mercifully brief. It wasn't easy for me then, and I am quite certain it would not be easy for me now to go back to school and homework again. Fortunately, I really liked our professors and soon found myself listening attentively to lectures and eager to learn more about the rehabilitation and care of paralytic, post-trauma patients like John C. and others I had cared for at St. Albans. In a way, former patients like John C. became a living laboratory in absentia and made learning easy for me.

An important part of the education and training of physical therapists in 1945 was the care and rehabilitation of poliomyelitis victims. The vaccine developed by Jonas Salk to prevent poliomyelitis had not yet burst upon the medical scene, and polio was likened to an epidemic, particularly among the very young. The very young sometimes included young soldiers and sailors, and we learned about hot packs to reduce muscle spasms during the acute phase of the disease, as well as the all-important retraining of muscles to prevent profound paralysis. Kinesiology, the science of human muscular movement, and Neurology, the branch of medicine dealing with the nervous system, were the most comprehensive and difficult courses we had, and Sam was our best and most important teacher. Sam was a cadaver. We gave him his name not out of disrespect, but as a constant reminder that he once was a living, breathing person, not just a mass of muscle, nerves, and blood vessels we were dissecting to learn how they worked.

But enough detail about our six months of nonstop lectures, rigorous training, and hands-on laboratory work that was rushing us along toward our six-month apprenticeship program and a subsequent assignment as nurse/physical therapist in the United States Navy. I learned first-hand during the process what I had always suspected, that all work, regardless of the perceived goal, with no time off for fun and relaxation, is both destructive in reaching the goal and unproductive for the person pursuing it. As course work pressures increased, I spent more and more time working with Mrs. Chappie in her garden, and I enjoyed many evenings playing cards and other table games with her. Her husband traveled for his company a good deal, and when he was away I frequently spent the evening talking with her about her home, her hobbies, bridge tournaments she played in, and Richmond society in general. I knew very little about southern customs, but I had already been privy to the ugly custom of black folk, for cause, pushing their way through a crowded bus to reach the back of the bus, and I wondered how she really felt about it. She had mentioned it once relative to our transportation needs, and I supposed at the time that it was meant to forewarn us. Mostly I avoided the topic, partly because I was essentially a guest in her home but mostly because our status as guests in the community was to end very soon.

In addition to her splendid garden, Mrs. Chappie's hobbies included an absolutely magnificent tropical fish tank that dominated one whole side of the family room. I spent many relaxing moments watching the beautiful angel fish floating majestically among the neon tetras, the black mollies, guppies, and other multicolored tropical fish. Many years later I read an article about such fish tanks being a useful tool in calming disturbed and psychotic patients, and I smiled as I remembered Mrs. Chappie's splendid fish tank and how I had used it to help me cope with the pressure of our crash course in Physical Therapy during that spring and summer in Richmond, Virginia.

Finally, it was August 16th. The course work was finished and the State Board Examination was over. I had passed, and while I did not ask, I assumed the other seventeen Navy nurses in the program did too. We were all tired and eager to get off for a few days leave before beginning our apprenticeship program. A graduation dinner and celebration had been planned to provide a short break for us with a two-day holiday trip to the Blue Ridge Mountains in North Carolina with our instructors. It was a delightful trip that included a tour of the Biltmore House and Gardens near Asheville. We had time off next day to do anything or nothing before the graduation dinner, and I learned another lesson. A splendid mountain lake near the Colonial Inn where we were staying looked inviting, and I decided to go for a swim. I had no idea how cold a mountain lake could be even in the middle of summer, and I shall never try that again. My swim was over the minute it started, and I spent the rest of the time before dinner huddled under a blanket.

With graduation festivities over, we were free to go our separate ways, and once again I headed west. Earlier we had been given an opportunity to choose between several Naval hospitals with a staff physiatrist (a physician specializing in physical therapy) aboard who would be in charge of our apprenticeship program. I chose and was assigned to the United States Naval Hospital in Corona, California. Here, while the shooting war was over, the war for a great many survivors was just beginning.

U.S. Naval Hospital, Corona: 18 August 1946–10 March 1947

In 1946 Corona, California was a sleepy little country town about thirty-five miles southeast of Los Angeles, nestled among the California foothills on one side and orange groves on the other. When last I visited the area, circa 1980, the orange groves had succumbed to the developer's axe, and Corona had become just another burgeoning California city/town.

After leaving Richmond, I spent a few days in Illinois visiting my parents before once again taking the train west out of Chicago, this time via the northern route to San Francisco and then on to Los Angeles. The train trip for me this time was a very different one. While I loved the grandeur of the Rocky Mountains, what I enjoyed most was making the trip aboard a train loaded with celebrating, happy travelers. The war was over, and many of the travelers were soldiers and sailors going home or just going west to make their homes there as so many ex-military personnel did after WWII. Not just a few fellow travelers on the train were still in uniform, and crap games were in full swing wherever space was available. Another Navy nurse, en route to San Francisco for duty, and I teamed up and joined in the fun on several occasions. As novices we had more than a normal share of luck. Losers were expected to pick up the check in the

31

diner, and perhaps it wasn't just luck because we seldom ate alone.

The train arrived in San Francisco only minutes before I was to catch the train for Los Angeles. I had very little time to see anything of San Francisco as I had hoped, but it really did not matter. The trip had been fun, but I had traveled many miles and many hours since leaving Richmond, and I was anxious to arrive in Corona, at the Navy Hospital, and in the room in the nurses' quarters that I would occupy for the next six months.

The Corona Hospital, before the Navy took it over, had been a "time-out" kind of get-away-from-it-all rest home and spa frequented primarily by affluent Hollywood gentry. The main building was an elegant hacienda-type building that sprawled across the top of a hill sloping gently down through a garden park to a small lake and boathouse. Naturally enough, after the Navy moved in and took over, the boathouse became the Officers Club and something of a haven for overworked doctors, nurses, and patients alike. After the first few weeks on the wards, I spent any time left over in the late afternoon sitting at the club on a narrow terrace overlooking the lake, watching the wild ducks and seagulls come skidding in over the water looking for a hand-out from whoever might be serving that afternoon. Usually it was George, a wise old gentleman who customarily wore his dentures in his shirt pocket, tended bar when the bar was open, and always had time to listen when anyone might have had a bad day and wanted to talk about it.

The Navy Hospital at Corona was said to have been a three-thousand-bed hospital in 1946, and perhaps it was. There were three separate sections, including a multiple-bed compound designed to handle patients with tuberculosis. Another section added by the Navy was much like the multiple barracks that served as a general hospital at Great Lakes. The third, of course, was the main hospital, described earlier as the former rest home and spa for Hollywood's affluent clientele. As one might expect, the Physical Therapy Department was located there with its indoor heated pool, massage and exercise rooms already available. Wards used to house and care for severely handicapped patients and polio victims with debilitating residual paralysis were also located in the main hospital for practical reasons, e.g., to accommodate wheelchair mobility for handicapped patients.

Of the first eighteen Navy nurses prepared at the Baruch Center to become Physical Therapy Technicians (a second group immediately followed our group there), six of us elected to serve our apprenticeship at Corona. Josie, my roommate in Richmond, Sarah, Norma, Clara, Maxine, and I were assigned rooms in the nurses' quarters, not now as a special group but as new nurses reporting in for duty, and I think we all were glad to feel we were once again part of the Navy Nurse Corps and expected to dress accordingly in our white duty uniforms and caps.

It was a bit of a scramble for me that first day to appear prepared for duty. A hot iron would have helped, but my starched white duty uniforms had been packed at the bottom of my footlocker for six months, long enough to look a bit yellow as well as a lot wrinkled. My first order of business after we were welcomed aboard by the chief nurse, who I thought at the time was not too sure she approved of us, and the physiatrist who obviously did approve, was to get my uniforms to the laundry. Dorrie, my kind roommate in the nurses' quarters, was a big help with that. She was a happy-go-lucky, don't-worry-about-it kind of person who knew and liked to chat with the civilian personnel on the compound, and I had a freshly washed, white and well-pressed duty uniform to wear the very next day.

About our patients, after introducing us to the staff in the Physical Therapy Department, the physiatrist, Dr. Rod (short for Rodney) as he was called by the patients apparently with his enthusiastic approval, took us on a tour of the wards to meet the patients we would be working with. We resembled, I think, a scene from a modern doctor-drama on television wherein a big-shot doctor strides authoritatively into a ward or patient's room with his retinue following meekly behind him. The big difference in the scenario here, however, was Dr. Rod, who smiled and exchanged jokes with the patients instead of poring over their charts and quizzing students or interns about how the patient is doing instead of asking the patient. I knew immediately that I would like and enjoy working with this fine doctor.

The tour of the wards over, we returned to the Physical Therapy Department to get acquainted with the staff and to get our one-on-one patient assignments. The staff included five enlisted personnel (two WAVES, three corpsmen) and two Registered Physical Therapy Technicians (RPTT). The chief therapist, looking forward to leaving the service on the point system, seemed glad enough to shed some of her responsibilities. Her assistant, however, was decidedly less enthusiastic about turning responsibility for patient treatments over to us. I wondered about that at the time, but decided I might resent it too if our positions were reversed and she seemed to be taking over my duties as a ward management nurse.

The first few weeks, we spent much of our time in the Physical Therapy Department proper doing routine treatments, diathermy, massage, hydrotherapy, muscle testing, therapeutic exercise, etc. Most of the patients we saw and worked with were either ambulatory or self-mobilized in a wheelchair. They were also men with minor injuries or postpolio disabilities waiting for final evaluation and discharge to their home or a veterans hospital. I was looking forward to working with patients on the wards, particularly the paralytic patients I had observed on the wards when making rounds with Dr. Rod. These were the survivors, the men who knew all about the "glory" of war, the men like John C. in St. Albans who wished he had died in the jungle with his buddies.

When my anticipated assignment on the wards was finally scheduled, it was to work with the patients on the poliomyelitis ward. While the patients there were paralytics, and many of them were indeed severely handicapped by the ravages of the disease, their treatment and rehabilitation procedures were very different from those used in the care and rehabilitation of paraplegic and other traumatic spinal cord injury cases. I shall not try to describe in detail the causes and effects of the disease. Instead I shall describe an incident on the ward with a severely handicapped patient that will explain something about poliomyelitis victims and my experiences working with them.

I cannot recall the young man's name, first or last, after all these years, but "Kilroy" comes to mind as a suitable alias in telling his story. The young man, a.k.a. "Kilroy" here, had been terribly ill with poliomyelitis shortly after enlisting in the Navy and had spent many months in a respirator (frequently referred to as an iron lung) just to stay alive. His arms and shoulder muscles were severely paralyzed. His back and leg muscles, however, were not affected by the disease. When I was assigned to the ward, Kilroy had already been allowed out of the respirator for a short time on a daily basis for muscle testing, retraining, and exercise. He was very popular among the other patients on the ward, and he got around in a lightweight aluminum wheelchair with the footrests removed. He propelled himself around with his feet, his badly atrophied and paralyzed arms and hands carefully placed and secured on the arms of the chair. Occasionally, when he was up, a corpsman would take him outside for a while, and Kilroy gradually spent more and more up-time visiting around the ward.

One day after his muscle retraining session, Kilroy disappeared. The ward nurse was looking for him; I was working with another patient, and the corpsmen said they had not seen him since they had helped him with lunch. We all thought he was probably just visiting on another ward. He had to be around somewhere in the hospital, and someone surely would remember seeing him because rolling along in his wheelchair propelled only by his feet, Kilroy mostly moved backward to go forward. We were convinced that he would show up sooner or later because he still slept in the respirator. It was like his security blanket, and he never went to bed without it.

None of us thought it worthwhile to look anywhere but around the hospital. I checked the Physical Therapy Department on the first floor. The ward nurse called around at the other wards to ask if anyone had seen him. The corpsman even looked outside where he sometimes took Kilroy. By late afternoon we were becoming increasingly concerned, and the ward nurse decided she had no choice but to call security. Shortly after she made the call, a cab rolled up to the main entrance of the hospital. The cabbie retrieved Kilroy's wheelchair from the trunk of his cab and carefully helped our missing patient into it. Security and everyone else who had spent the better part of the afternoon looking for Kilroy did not know whether to laugh or to cry. Where had he been? It was easy enough to tell that he had been in a bar somewhere, but how did he get there?

When we got Kilroy back to the ward, fed, and sobered up a bit, he told us it was simple. He rolled up the road to the main gate, yakked a bit with the guard on duty and then rolled on through when the guard was not looking. After that, he simply coasted down the hill toward Corona. Someone had told him about a bar at the bottom of the hill, so he just rolled on into it, convinced the bartender that it was okay for him to have a drink if he wanted one, and the bartender gave him several beers before the locals from the orange groves showed up. Then they all had a ball. Afterward the "guys" called the cab, and that was how he got back to the hospital.

Discipline Kilroy? Certainly he was AWOL (Absent Without Leave), and security had been called.

"No way!" said Dr. Rod with a grin. "The kid deserved a break. Besides, after he gets over his hangover, he'll probably be better for it."

Dr. Rod was right. Kilroy did have a bad hangover. I never heard, but I expect it was the guard at the gate, not Kilroy, who had some explaining to do to security about the incident at the gate.

My next assignment was on the paraplegic wards, but before describing my experiences there, a pause here may be warranted. While still stationed at St. Albans, I had signed over from the Naval Reserve to the regular Navy (from U.S. Navy Nurse Corps, USNR to U.S. Navy Nurse Corps, USN), partly to enhance my chance of being accepted for the Physical Therapy course and college credit toward a Bachelor of Science degree, and partly because the war was officially over, and I still hoped for an opportunity to travel abroad. September 18, 1946, the Medical Officer in Command at Corona made it official and swore me into the Regular Navy Nurse Corps.

My experiences on the paraplegic wards got started off with a bang. When I walked confidently into the ward, eager to go to work, I was very nearly run down by a speeding wheelchair. It was an accident, of course, but the ward nurse assured me, "It happens a lot around here. These guys are lousy drivers." She was laughing, but she was also serious, and I found out why very quickly. Every patient on the ward who was able to be up, or could be if he felt like it, had his own wheelchair parked within easy reach at his bedside. At first I wondered about that, but Dr. Rod reminded me that the profound paralysis of the muscles below the level of a spinal cord injury sustained by a patient causes the skin over those muscles to break down and bedsores to develop unless some significant movement is somehow maintained.

A paraplegic patient who is able to be up is encouraged to be up, and a wheelchair at his disposal is a valuable tool to enhance such encouragement. A bribe of sorts, perhaps, but motivation toward mobility is the primary goal in the overall care and rehabilitation of paraplegic patients. The ultimate goal, for which motivation and mobility are the necessary first steps, is the ability of the patient to cope with the disability, and then to go on to work within the parameters of the disability toward independent movement and living, if possible in a home environment.

While I had been told which patients I was to work with on that particular ward (there were two such wards), I could readily see which patients needed attention. The one in the speeding wheelchair certainly was not one of them. Neither was the patient right behind him in a race to wherever they were going at 8:30 in the morning. Looking down the long row of patient beds on either side of the ward, it occurred to me that this was not the time for me to be standing around wondering where to begin. First step was to find the patients on my assignment list and get on with their care and my day. That day was to be my kind of day for the next eighteen months, and I have never worked harder nor felt better about it either before or since.

Our six-month apprenticeship assignment was over in March, and once again we were given a choice between several duty stations for our next assignment. My choice once again was easily made. I chose to stay on at Corona, partly because I liked California but mostly because I liked working with the patients on the paraplegic wards. In February it was official. My orders read:

SUBJECT; "CHANGE OF DUTY"

1. Upon completion of six months' apprenticeship in Physical Therapy and when directed by the Medical Officer in Command, Naval Hospital, on or about 1 March 1947, you will regard yourself detached from duty at the Naval Hospital, Corona, Calif., and from such other duty as may have been assigned you; will report to the Medical Officer in Command, Naval Hospital, Corona, Calif., for duty as Physical Therapist and for such other duty as may be assigned you.

2. You are hereby authorized to delay for a period of 15 days in reporting in compliance with these orders, such delay to count as leave; . . . .

My orders, delivered to me dated 10 March 1947, made it clear.

1. Delivered. Detached this date.

2. You are directed to vacate Government Quarters this date.

As written, my orders seemed to say I was to be detached from duty at Corona Naval Hospital and subsequently reattached for duty at Corona Naval Hospital fifteen days later. That, of course, was exactly what happened. I had to vacate the nurses' quarters, to pack up all my personal belongings (my duty uniforms, extra clothing, books, pictures, etc.) and store them somewhere off the base for fifteen days, then be reassigned to nurses' quarters, retrieve my duty uniforms and other belongings, and be reassigned for duty as physical therapist and for such other duty as may be assigned.

The "such other duty" I was to discover later meant week-end and night duty nursing assignments at the discretion of the chief nurse for those of us who had opted for and been reassigned for duty at the Corona Naval Hospital.

All this seemed a great bother, but the fifteen days leave was most welcome. I had been looking forward to making a trip back to New York to see a Naval Air Cadet I had been dating while still at St. Albans and with whom I had been carrying on a kind of pen-pal relationship. Perhaps my biological clock was ticking, or maybe it was because many of my nurse friends, back-home family members, and acquaintances were either married, or planning to be, and I wanted to see if any of that "old black magic" was involved in my relationship with Fritz. It wasn't.

Fritz met me at the airport in New York on crutches, wearing a toe-to-knee plaster cast on one leg. "A skiing accident!" It was bitterly cold and beginning to rain. The roads would be icy, and Fritz was worried about getting home. I was wondering how long I might be stuck in this miserable climate after leaving the lovely balmy weather in California. That old black magic was only a few words in a then popular song after all. We took a cab into Manhattan, not saying very much because there didn't seem much to say. I checked in at the Hotel Commodore, a still popular "watering hole" for the military, probably because of its convenient location and connection via the indoor walkway into Grand Central Station. We had a quick drink at the bar, a friendly chat over dinner about our various plans and recent activities, and got Fritz safely to the upstate train on time. I was never quite sure if he was as relieved about ending our might-have-been romance as I was, but a postage stamp and a "Dear Fritz" letter would certainly have been a lot cheaper for both of us.

A good night's sleep, after the chaos of getting packed, stowing my gear, having a few drinks at the club and a chat with old George, reporting to the commanding officer to get detached from the hospital, and hitching a ride on a military flight out of March Field bound for New York, helped make the second day of my fifteen-day leave a little brighter. A change from a badly wrinkled uniform into fresh clothing, followed by a country-style breakfast of grits (which I learned to like in Richmond), ham and eggs, a muffin, and coffee, helped even more, and I realized any regrets I might have about the failed romance were already behind me. I was relieved.

I was in New York City, one of my favorite places to be, and I was looking forward to spending some time with my brother, a former chaplain and Lt(jg) in the Navy then going to Columbia University on the GI Bill. Brother "Bun," so nicknamed by our dad and still so-called by his siblings, had a walk-up bachelor apartment on West 11th Street in Greenwich Village. Not surprising, brother Bun was busy at the university most of the day, but we got together several times over lunch or dinner for a family visit, and once for a night at the theater to see a popular new musical playing on Broadway called "Oklahoma." Then Joe, a native New Yorker and a friend of my brother at the university, decided I should not leave New York City without first enjoying a New York style lobster dinner. It was a first time adventure for me wrestling with a hand-selected, well-prepared Maine lobster flown in fresh from the sea, and it was indeed a delicious experience.

Joe had chosen an uptown, East Side restaurant called "The King of the Sea" for the occasion. The decor wasn't great, but the lobster was, and I soon found myself up to my necktie in lobster claws dripping with melted butter. A grinning, observant waitress brought me an adult size bib to make my attack on the luckless lobster a little less

41

messy. I enjoyed it. So, too, did Joe, along with a few other diners in the restaurant who apparently enjoyed watching an obvious amateur in a Navy uniform don a large bib to renew an attack on the claws of an already defenseless lobster. It was still a messy business, but it was a fun evening, and I think even the chef enjoyed it. Joe got the check, of course. I got the bib, a fresh one, compliments of the chef, and somewhere among my favorite things I still have the bib, the bright red letters across the front spelling out "The King of the Sea." Many years and more than a few lobster dinners later, when I was then living and working in New York City, I tried to find that well-remembered restaurant, but The King of the Sea just wasn't there any more, and no one I talked to even remembered it ever had been.

The month of March in New York City is mostly still winter, with occasional thaws followed by snow or rain, rendering the streets and sidewalks slippery, or sloppy, and usually both. A few days of this with nothing much to do can get a little boring, even in that sophisticated, exciting city. In 1947 the war really was over in New York City. You could feel it in the streets, see it in the blank, unseeing faces of New Yorkers rushing from wherever to whatever, and hear it in the cha-ching of the cash registers in all the stores along Fifth Avenue. Postwar New York was too busy if one did not go out to a job and had nothing much to do, and I decided to catch the next train for Chicago and to spend the rest of my leave at home.

It was winter in Chicago too when I arrived there, but I spent two days talking nonstop with my married sister (Ione) and her family before catching a Trailways bus for the down-state trip to my parents' home. After my family visit with my brother in New York, I was looking forward to seeing three other brothers also home from the war and already getting settled into their postwar occupations. Dr. Richard, former major in the Army Medical Corps, was busy setting up his practice in Galesburg, Illinois. Cpl. Ernest and his wife Leta, with their small son Donald, were getting settled in a job in Bloomington, Illinois, and Sgt. Emile, home from Calcutta and the China-Burma-India run with the Army Air Corps, was now married to Jean, his hometown sweetheart and pen pal all during the war. They were both busy at the University of Illinois preparing to become teachers. Two other brothers and a sister were at home helping Mom and Dad on the farm. All the postwar activity made me restless and anxious to get back to my patients, the veterans of World War II.

U.S. Naval Hospital Corona: 25 March 1947–11 May 1948

Right on time I reported back to the Corona Naval Hospital, this time for duty as nurse-physical therapist. For the most part, my leave had been a pleasant one, but I was glad to be back and was looking forward to getting back to work. I was also glad to find I had been assigned the same room and roommate in the nurses' quarters that I had had during our apprenticeship program. Dorrie had become a good friend, and I was glad to be sharing a room with her again. I couldn't help thinking, however, what a bother it was to have to retrieve my sea chest (so-called by the base carpenter Dorrie had talked into making for me earlier) from storage and to go through the tiresome business of unpacking and getting my duty uniforms presentable after being away for only two weeks. The necessity, of course, was obvious. Dorrie might well have gotten orders or been assigned a new roommate while I was away. I might have been delayed getting back, my orders changed, or assigned to a different room and roommate, but none of that had happened, and I was content enough about being back that it didn't really matter.

With our apprenticeship program over, we were once again Navy nurses reporting now to the chief nurse instead of only to physiatrist, Dr. Rod. Clara, better known to her friends as "Bunny," had chosen to be reassigned to

Corona too, probably because she eventually married the Mr. Wonderful she met there during our apprenticeship program. Our duties as physical therapists did not change significantly, except for the "such other duty as may be assigned you" clause in our orders that I mentioned earlier. Reporting to the chief nurse, we were regarded as nursing staff and were no longer excused from weekend duty and normal rotation to night duty on the wards.

Weekend duty for me was no great problem since I enjoyed having a day off during the week to go into Long Beach or Los Angeles shopping. The rules about dress uniforms had finally changed. We were now permitted to wear civilian clothes off duty, and a whole new wardrobe was very much on my mind. We also were now permitted to have a car on the base, but that required considerable patience and carefully hoarded savings to own one.

A new car in 1947 was at a premium, not because of the price tag but because it was gone almost before it left the factory. Detroit had been busy turning out either luxury cars or tractor trucks and tanks for the military during the war years and had not caught up with the demand for small cars by GI Joe and Jane coming home from military service. For me a new car could and would have to wait. A new wardrobe did not have to, and I felt very elegant indeed after a midweek shopping trip in Long Beach where I bought a fashionable and very feminine new suit with a pair of high-heeled shoes and a knockout hat to match.

Night duty on the wards was quite a different matter. My old problem of staying awake while nearly everyone else was sleeping, including the patients, had not gotten better. The wards at Corona were bigger, and the patients for the most part were sicker than those we cared for in the dispensary at the Naval Air Station in Glenview, but the distractions available were far less rewarding. For me, night duty in the military environment was much like being on guard duty.

One marched up a long ward, paused to listen, turned, and marched back down the ward, paused to listen again, then repeated the process until relieved. There seldom was anything serious to break the monotony until one night during my first tour of night duty at Corona the medics brought in a profoundly comatose patient who apparently had had a massive stroke. The patient had been admitted to the hospital and arrived on my ward with no file, no orders for care, and no information about him other than that he had been flown in from Las Vegas because he was a veteran and there was no place else close by to take him.

After the medics left, I checked the patient's vital signs. He was an old man, not at all like the young men we were used to. His hair was sparse and gray, no teeth, skinny arms and legs suggesting poor nutrition, and I wondered why he had been sent there and by whom. What had he been doing in Las Vegas? Surely there was a hospital there that could have cared for him. We did not even know his name or whether his family had been notified. The doctor on duty was equally mystified and told me he would let me know what he could find out.

Seven o'clock (0700) came, and the day nurse arrived. Our John Doe was still alive and still comatose. All I knew that I hadn't known earlier was why he was brought to Corona. With the Corona Hospital's patient population shrinking as patients were being discharged either to their home or to a veterans hospital, the Corona Naval Hospital had begun accepting local veterans for emergency care until other arrangements could be made for them.

Apparently, our John Doe was deemed unlikely to survive his stroke and was sent to us for treatment in case he did. Unfortunately, his personal effects, wallet, watch, clothing, etc., plus a medical record if one existed, got lost in the shuffle somewhere between Las Vegas in Nevada and Corona in California. He was still John Doe and still comatose when I arrived for duty on the ward the following night. I wondered what if anything we could do for him and asked the doctor on duty if he thought it wise to start passive motion on arms and legs to relieve muscle spasms likely to occur when and if he did wake up.

We had discussed such therapy during our course work in Richmond, and this seemed a good opportunity for me to find out if it worked. We had also talked about how much a comatose patient might hear and comprehend of what was said and done around him or her by caregivers, friends, and relatives. The doctor agreed, "It might help, and it can't hurt, so go ahead, do anything you can for him."

So began a small research and learning project for me that not only helped solve my night duty problems staying awake, but taught me a lesson that I have never forgotten in all the years since WWII. A comatose patient may not be able to respond, but he or she just might be able to hear. Each night when I came on duty I took my John Doe patient through passive range-of-motion exercises on arms and legs, talking quietly to him about anything I thought might stimulate some response. One night when I had begun to wonder whether John Doe would ever wake up, I realized his eyes were open, and he was glaring up at me as I moved his arm up and over his head. I spoke to him calmly, asked if his arm hurt, how he felt, and what his name was. I explained that he was in a hospital and that I was moving his arms and legs so that they would not get stiff. Finally I asked him to try to squeeze my hand. His only response was "God damn!"

The next night it was "God damn" to every question asked, and I knew then that he was aphasic, that he probably understood, but that the brain damage from the stroke had destroyed his ability to speak normally. I had worked with hemiplegic (stroke) patients on occasion as a student nurse and knew that speech therapy was a long, drawn-out process that may or may not help a stroke-related aphasia. John Doe could not even tell us his name.

We did learn our John Doe's name eventually, of course. And we did locate his eyeglasses and dentures after I bedeviled a somewhat reluctant sister and nephew who finally showed up, and were far more interested in what had happened to a diamond ring he habitually wore than in finding out what had happened to the rest of his personal effects. I never learned what really happened in Las Vegas, why his wallet never showed up, or why it took several weeks before his next of kin eventually did, but only to insist there was no way they could take care of him at home. I could only guess what might have happened to the diamond ring they were so concerned about or to the wallet they never mentioned. I shall let you as an interested reader surmise, as I did, that our John Doe's gambling habits had not endeared him to the members of his own family.

My tour of night duty while working with John Doe proved more interesting than usual, but I was glad enough when it was time to return to my physical therapy assignment, working with paralytic patients on the wards. I did look in on John Doe from time to time for the next few weeks, until he was up and shuffling along using an old-fashioned, high-backed, wooden wheelchair as a sort of crutch when he wasn't sitting in it. I assumed then that he would go home sooner or later or be transferred to a veterans hospital to work with a speech therapist. Unfortunately, neither solution for his multiple problems was to occur. I learned much later, after I had been transferred back to Great Lakes to head up the Physical Therapy Department there, that our John Doe patient somehow managed to open a window on the sixth floor of the hospital and solved his multiple problems by dropping six floors to his death.

The war with Japan was officially over September 2, 1945, but the war was still far from over for the many survivors still on the wards at the Corona Naval Hospital. The war was not yet over for me, either. True, the shooting had stopped, and the country was gearing up for the economic boom years ahead, but the future did not look very bright or hold much promise for the veterans still languishing in military hospitals, waiting for whatever future was in store for them.

There was very little the young men on the paralytic wards could hope for relative to recovering from their paralyses or for regaining any significant use of paralyzed extremities without supportive prostheses or braces. Most of them had been in one or another military hospital for many months living with hope and knew they had almost no chance of living a normal life, of having their own home, a wife and children, a job, a future. Many of them were bitter. Some of them were angry; others were simply cynical or caustic, saying in effect, "Why bother? The doc says I'll probably spend the rest of my life in a wheelchair anyway; so why bother?" Still others, while they understood and accepted their disabilities as permanent, insisted there was no point in coping with braces and crutches or even trying to become a little more independent. "What for?"

I shall admit, sometimes after a long day I wondered about the "what for" too, but after a walk in the garden down to the lake to watch the wild ducks skidding in for a handout, I knew what for. It was my job to do whatever necessary to help these patients cope with their disabilities and to work toward some degree of independence and mobility. During the nearly eighteen months I was stationed at the Corona Naval Hospital (September 1946 to May 1948), the greatest challenge for me was working with the paraplegic patients. Caring for such patients is quite different from caring for hemiplegic (post CVA or stroke) patients and poliomyelitis patients. Simply stated, the difference is relevant or related to the kind and location of the trauma to the central nervous system sustained by the patient as a result of disease or injury to his brain and/or spinal cord. Paralysis in the hemiplegia patient is characterized by weakness on one side of the patient's body, and treatment during the acute phase focuses on the cause. Therapy may or may not be feasible, based on the overall physical condition of the patient.

Paralysis sustained by the poliomyelitis patient may not occur at all, or it may involve multiple muscle groups, rendering the patient severely handicapped. Now known to be caused by a virus, treatment initially focuses on the disease. Subsequent muscle retraining and rehabilitation therapy, if needed, follows the acute phase of the disease and usually is uncomplicated by the physical ups and downs suffered by quadriplegic and paraplegic patients. The frequent and so-called physical ups and downs suffered by quadriplegic and paraplegic patients are usually directly related to the level and degree of damage to the patient's spinal cord, and such damage for these patients is usually a result of an accident, a fall, a bullet wound, flying debris from a bomb, a motorcycle or automobile accident, etc.

The quadriplegic patient, for example, usually has suffered a crushing injury to one or more cervical vertebrae, resulting in damage to his spinal cord. After such an injury, profound paralysis occurs in both internal body functions and all four extremities. Similarly, the paraplegic patient will have suffered an injury to vertebrae and spinal cord in the thoracic or lumbar area of his spine, with resulting paralysis directly related to the level of the injury and the degree of damage to the spinal cord and nerves that control the lower half of his body. Both such patients develop recurring pressure sores and bladder infections that are difficult to control. Treatments, therefore, become somewhat erratic with the need to cope with the patient's frequent infections, bedsores, and respiratory, urinary, and other internal body functions.

Because a paraplegic patient's arms and upper body remain essentially functional, the patient has greater mobility and thus will have fewer of the ups and downs in treatment than the largely immobile quadriplegic patient. The most difficult problem for both patients, however, is a personal problem. Both are rendered impotent as well as incontinent by their paralyses, and the will to live, to hope for a future, becomes increasingly difficult for such patients to retain. Working with them is not easy. Dealing with their multifaceted problems can be overwhelming, not only for the patient, but for the therapist who must somehow restore a measure of hope for the future before any healing and progress toward rehabilitation can begin. It was this challenge, I think, that made working with the paraplegic patients at Corona the high point in my Navy career.

The concept of holistic medicine in the 1940s and '50s was still more concept than practice, but treating the whole patient rather than just his disease or disabilities was mandatory and became the modus operandi in caring for the paralytic patients at Corona Naval Hospital. Dr. Rod, a fine physician and surgeon who became concerned about the proliferation of bedsores and infection among the patients on the paraplegic wards, decided to do something about it. He got permission from the commanding officer to open the gymnasium in the main hospital, which was being used only sparingly by the medical staff, to wheelchair patients and requisitioned several basketballs for their use. He hoped this would not only generate greater mobility and muscle control for them, and thus fewer bedsore episodes, but would also provide added incentive to exercise regularly and a healthy kind of entertainment as well.

The gymnasium program for the paralytic patients generated so much interest among the patients and was so successful that the medical staff soon became interested in the program and began dropping by the gymnasium to watch

51

and applaud. Eventually from this therapeutic exercise program one of the first, if not the first, wheelchair basketball teams began to emerge. After the patients found a sometime (non-professional) coach on the base who could help get their team organized, even more interest and participation in the program were generated among the patients. When the doctors were challenged and accepted the challenge to compete with the patients in a real game on their level (the doctors to be confined to a wheelchair too), the enthusiasm generated knew no bounds.

At first the idea of the staff doctors playing competitive basketball with the paraplegic patients seemed too dangerous, even with the handicap the doctors had agreed to, and the doctors would still have an unfair advantage. But the anticipated game had become too important to the patients for the staff to call it off. The paraplegic wards were literally abuzz with excitement. Even the quadriplegics were enthusiastic and were talking about how they could find a way to get to the game. Suddenly, we were seeing our patients beginning to feel like men, not like cripples waiting around to be sent to a veterans hospital for the rest of their lives, or worse, home to become an object of pity and a burden to their families. It was 1947, the peace treaty with the Japanese had long since been signed, and the patients were well aware the Bureau of Naval Personnel was busy reviewing service records and that sooner or later a disability discharge would be forthcoming for them.

The doctors vs patients wheelchair basketball game proved a great morale booster for the patients. Certainly it was not so for the doctors, who bumbled and fumbled the ball, crashed into each other and the walls, and were soundly defeated. Watching the game, it was quite evident that a wheelchair is not as maneuverable as it seemed to be when a paraplegic patient was getting around in one. I admit I was feeling a little sorry for the bruised and somewhat battered doctors after the game, but most of the hospital staff was rooting for the patients, and I was delighted when they won.

Life was not quite the same on the paraplegic wards after the game. In subtle ways the patients seemed more confident, as though they had somehow proved to themselves if not yet to anyone else that they could succeed at something, and that just maybe, if they really tried they might be able to make some kind of a life for themselves after their discharge from the hospital.

The challenge was there, and the next hurdle for our paraplegic patients was learning to drive a specially modified car with gear shift, brakes, accelerator, etc., built into the steering column. This special program for handicapped veterans got underway at Corona in the fall of 1947, and we used it much like a bribe, getting our paraplegic patients to work out daily strengthening their upper bodies and arms so that they could manage their own basic care, e.g., bathing, dressing, putting on their leg braces, getting themselves down to the exercise room to work out, and to practice walking between the parallel bars. All this self-help activity, of course, had a double objective and was leading up to learning to get around on crutches using a so-called swing-through, three-point gait—not an easy accomplishment for even the strongest and most determined patients among them.

Driving the special car modified for handicapped patients' use requires considerably more than simply learning to manage the brakes and giving it the gas. First the patient must learn to get into the car, usually from a fold-up type wheelchair. Then he must be able to safely lean down to fold up the chair and stow it safely behind his seat at the wheel before he even puts the key in the ignition. After that he must also learn, or better said re-learn, to drive the car using only his hands and arms to control starting, stopping, steering. As one might guess, the process of learning to re-learn to drive without foot and leg control of brakes and gas pedal can be a pretty harrowing experience. And so it was for not just a few of our paraplegic patients who eventually decided to settle for their wheelchairs to get around and to leave the driving to someone else.

One of my well remembered and star paraplegic patients at Corona was Pete (his real name), who not only relearned to drive the modified car successfully, but eventually went on to graduate from UCLA (University of California at Los Angeles) and even appeared briefly as a patient in the film *The Men,* a movie starring Marlon Brando playing the part of a paraplegic coping with the everyday problems of a handi-capped veteran. All this, of course, happened after Pete was honorably discharged from the service and transferred to the veterans hospital in Ventura, California. I lost track of him after his discharge and transfer, but by chance I saw the film he was in, in a little theater in Waukegan, Illinois, while I was still in the Navy and heading up the Physical Therapy Department at Great Lakes Naval Hospital. His picture and the story when he graduated from UCLA I saw later when it appeared in *Life* magazine. Now, after all these years I still wonder about Pete, where he is and what he is doing.

Pete was one of my special patients at Corona. I met him soon after his arrival on the paraplegic ward. I don't remember, if indeed I ever knew, what happened to him, but I did know he was a very angry and bitter young man who wasn't very popular among the corpsmen or among the other patients on the ward. He wasn't very popular at first with me, either, when I paused at his bedside to say good morning and to introduce myself. In fact, in essence he told me to get lost, or words to that effect, cleaned up considerably here for reader consumption. I did oblige him for a few days, then Dr. Rod called me aside during rounds one day and suggested ". . . do whatever you have to do to get this guy moving, or he'll end up with a bedsore on his butt that won't quit."

Dr. Rod was right, of course, and I wondered at the time how exactly I was to accomplish getting this angry young man moving. His bed had the usual overhead trapeze and bar equipment designed to help a paraplegic patient change his position in bed and to move from his bed to a wheelchair. His shoes with leg braces attached, along with a duffel bag and his personal effects, had arrived on the ward soon after he did. He also had a hospital-issue robe and some of his own clothing available at his bedside. Why then was he still so angry and uncivil to anyone trying to help him? Deep denial? Probably, but more likely perhaps some serious trauma to his self-esteem.

Pete was a handsome young man in his early twenties, and any young man in his prime surely would suffer great anguish and loss of self-esteem when forced by circumstances to accept the role of an impotent cripple with little or no hope of recovery. What then was the best way to deal with so much anger and to rekindle some hope for this angry young man?

After thinking it over, I decided if Pete was indeed immersed in self-pity and denial as he seemed to be, the best approach in a rehabilitation program for him had to be both authoritative and challenging. A friendly "let me help" approach probably would prove more destructive than constructive, and depending on the extent of his paralysis, what he could do or should eventually be able to do for himself, he must be challenged to do without discussion or debate. I had learned earlier working with handicapped patients that the "Oh, you poor boy, let me help," or a rush to help without being asked, often annoyed the handicapped person rather than helped him.

And so began Pete's rehabilitation battles, not just with me or to avoid the threatened bedsore on his backside, but to learn to live and accept a whole new way of life and living. It was not easy. The first few weeks he spent fussing and cussing about bed exercise, about learning how to move safely from the bed to a wheelchair and back again, and just about everything else I told him he must do. Then one day when I arrived on the ward he was up, dressed in fresh pajamas, and sitting in a wheelchair grinning from ear to ear. One of the corpsmen on the ward had helped get him into a shower stall and hosed him down. He had had a bath, a real bath, and he was ready for whatever came next.

The next, I decided, should be a day off to get acquainted with some of the other men on the ward. He needed to listen to and swap a few stories with "the guys," the men who could teach him to laugh at a joke again, the men who would share life with him while he was still in the Corona Naval Hospital and probably later in a veterans hospital as well.

The next step for Pete was working out on a mat in the exercise room using weights to build up his strength in arms and shoulder muscles in preparation for the most difficult part of his rehabilitation program, learning to get around with braces on crutches.

Pete enjoyed working out on the mat. He even began to like wearing his leg braces, which allowed him to stand on his feet while working out in the parallel bars. Every step of his program became a challenge. He even joined "the guys" playing basketball in the gym during their practice sessions. After a while, nothing was too difficult. Everything was a challenge for Pete, until he tried the swing-through gait on crutches. He could do it easily in the parallel bars, but with only the unstable crutches to hang on to, he wasn't very brave. It was then I offered the carrot on the stick. I reminded him that he would need to be able to use his crutches if he wanted to learn to drive the modified car and hoped eventually to own one. He just sprawled in his wheelchair and stared up at me as though I was out of my mind. Was I serious? I wondered about that myself at the time. I had no control over who might be deemed qualified or even considered for the "Cars for the Handicapped" program. Pete's responses to a challenge, however, suggested he would, if he could, go on not only to drive a modified car but might even one day go on to own one.

I didn't see a lot of Pete after that. In May, Dr. Rod requested a temporary leave for me to attend a three-day "Symposium on Supervision" at the Baruch Center of Physical Medicine, at the Medical College of Virginia in Richmond. Temporary leave (May 26–30) was granted, and I flew into Washington DC via Naval Air Transport service out of March Field on 22 May 1947. My sojourn in our nation's capital was brief, and I decided, before catching the train for Richmond, that someday I would come back to spend some quality time in that fascinating city when I could stay longer. I did in 1953 as a physical therapist at the Kabat Kaiser Institute for Neurological Diseases then located on 16th Street.

My assignment when I got back to Corona on June 3 had changed somewhat. I did not get a raise or a promotion, but I did inherit the departing supervisor's job in the Physical Therapy Department. The part I liked most about my new responsibilities was that I was now no longer required to take my turn working night shifts and weekends, and I decided now was the time for me to buy a car.

Buying a car in the fall of 1947 was a very different process from the multiple-choice selection process we have today. Then, the demand for new, small personal cars by ex-service men and women settling on the West Coast far exceeded the supply. During the war years, Detroit had been busy turning out tanks and jeeps and big luxury cars for VIP politicians and generals, and automakers had not yet caught up with the growing demand for small cars. Nevertheless, one day I took myself off to the bank, converted my savings account to a checking account, and headed the following Saturday to East Los Angeles and Motor Miracle Mile. The dealer there was duly sympathetic and offered to put my name on a long waiting list for a new car. When I didn't seem too enthusiastic about that, he went on to suggest I might be interested in a used car. "A nice, clean little car came in just a few days ago . . . ." So, suddenly I was looking at and interested in a 1946 Dodge coupé without a scratch and looking very much like it may have spent much of the last two years up on blocks in a garage somewhere. Of course, I should have asked the pertinent "who, what, when, where," questions about the Dodge's history. And, of course, today I would neither have bought the first car I looked at, nor failed to ask pertinent questions of the dealer about whatever car I might seriously be looking at. But trust, in those early post-World War II days, was not just an idle word or condition among fellow Americans, and I trusted the dealer had treated me fairly when I handed him my check and happily drove my old/new car off the lot. What I failed to do and should certainly have done without being reminded was to check the gasoline gauge, and that foolish failure nearly ruined my day.

It was late afternoon when I drove my new/old Dodge coupé off the used car lot. It was roughly forty miles back to Corona, and having studied a map the dealer gave me, I thought I knew how to get back to the hospital without going back into downtown Los Angeles. But somewhere along the road I took I missed the turnoff onto Route 71 and drove four or five miles out of the way before turning back. At about the same time I remembered to look at the gas gauge. The needle was swaying gently back and forth over empty, and there wasn't a gas station or a town in sight. What to do? An easy question, of course. I had no choice. It was drive on with my fingers crossed until I ran out of gas or found a gas station still open. In those days gas stations were few and very far between for cause, and those still open for business closed early. Either my little old Dodge was running on air or my guardian angel was riding in the back seat that evening. I got back to the road to Corona and up the hill into the hospital parking lot before the needle on the gasoline gauge finally settled firmly on empty.

The next day my guardian angel took leave and Lady Luck took over. My roommate, Dorrie, called a friend who worked in maintenance. Of course he had a good laugh at my expense but came up with a gallon of gas so that I could get my illegally parked car out of the hospital parking lot (To park there I needed a security permit) and down the hill into Corona to find a gas station likely to be open on Sunday. After that my little old Dodge traveled somewhere nearly every weekend and sometimes, on a moonlit night, just for a relaxing drive through the orange groves. I still love the wonderful aroma of orange blossoms, but in that area the groves are mostly all gone now, replaced by small towns and major new highways. Route 91, once an easy-driving country highway between Riverside, Corona, and downtown Los Angeles, is now a smog-shrouded, busy, six-lane, bumper-to-bumper highway with multiple on/off ramps into small towns and cities along the way, a not-fun drive for commuters, I'm sure. Route 71, to the best of my knowledge, however, is still a two-lane, paved road winding up through the foothills to Interstate 10 and Route 101 into Pasadena and the Santa Anita Racetrack. I didn't get home for Christmas that year, but I did get to Pasadena for the Rose Bowl Parade. A little later I also got to the races at Santa Anita, but that is a whole different story about another important lesson I needed to learn. "Pay Attention to Where You Park Your Car, Dummy!" I was very nearly the last one out of the parking lot at the Santa Anita Racetrack one afternoon before Dorrie and I found my car parked right where I left it.

The winter and spring of 1947–48 were happy times for me. Dorrie and I took off whenever she had a free weekend for such places as San Bernardino and Lake Arrowhead to play in the snow, to Long Beach or Los Angeles to shop, or to one of my favorite places, a popular, old and delightful Mission Inn in Riverside, where we drank what they called a "Moscow Mule" served in a chilled copper mug and chatted with the locals.

Meanwhile, the war-time traffic was winding down at the Corona Naval Hospital. Disability discharge and transfer orders began arriving daily for our handicapped patients, and the second wave of Navy nurse physical therapy graduates who came to Corona for their apprenticeship program had gone on to their next duty assignments. By spring, my professional responsibilities had dwindled down to just a few. Pete was gone. Frank (not his real name) was still struggling with braces and crutches. With Frank, who was a fairly recent arrival on the paraplegic ward, I knew soon after his arrival that I could honestly promise him he could walk out of the hospital one day if he would just get off his backside, stop feeling sorry for himself, and get started working out seriously with his braces in the parallel bars.

Frank's rehabilitation program was not significantly different from Pete's program or from that of many of the other patients on the ward, but his spinal cord injury had been lower and less traumatic. Thus his paralysis was less profound. I knew from the medical records that came to the ward with him that he could, if he would, learn to get around on crutches using the swing-through, three-point gait, and that he might even get a little more control and use of his legs. He did get more control, and he was able to walk with the aid of braces and crutches. Before he left he said thank you with a beautifully carved and highly polished miniature Laughing Buddha statuette that he had gotten somewhere before he got hurt. It was a very special gift that he insisted

I take because, he said, he really wanted me to have it. I still have that handsome statuette, and I still cherish it, but I also still wonder why he would willingly have parted with it. Perhaps he bought it for some young lady back home who wrote a "Dear John" letter when she learned he had been badly hurt and would probably be crippled for the rest of his life.

"Dear John" letters happened often enough to our paraplegic patients. Sometimes it was better so, better that they did happen than to have a formerly devoted young lady, a fiancée, or even a wife insist on a marriage that did not and could not work because the wife could not accept or learn to cope with the reality of her husband's problems. True, the Dear John letter sometimes was a devastating blow for the paraplegic patient, but other times it actually became a profound relief for him as well. Marriage was a different kind of problem for paraplegic patients. It was one that eventually had to be dealt with, first by the attending physician, usually by Dr. Rod when the young lady or wife involved came to visit her husband or fiancé, then by a special prearranged session with a psychiatric counselor who was urged to brutally discuss individually and collectively with both parties the special problems such a marriage would entail.

By March of 1948 the professional activities for the medical staff at Corona were dwindling down, and many of the younger doctors were counting points and looking forward to leaving the service to set up their private practices elsewhere. Even Dr. Rod was counting points, and weeks, until he could leave and go home to his wife in San Francisco and to set up his private practice there. Word from my mother about happenings at home, about weddings, births, new homes and jobs, back to school projects, etc., for friends and siblings made me restless too. An era was ending, and I had made no plans for the future. There was no problem about being out of a job. I had signed over officially from

61

the Navy Reserve (USNR) to regular Navy (USN), 12 November 1947, at a time when the challenge of working with the handicapped and the California climate combined to make me feel this was what I wanted to do and where I wanted to do it. Another important lesson learned. Things change.

The war really was over, and the life and times in America were changing rapidly. I felt left behind with little of real challenge or interest to do. Dorrie was still at Corona, but her problems were somewhat different from mine. She had wanted to marry the doctor she was dating, but for whatever reason, he neglected to mention matrimony when his discharge came through, and he left without even suggesting they keep in touch. Dorrie was not happy, and eventually she began dating a corpsman, an enlisted man on her ward, and that was a no-no then just as it is now. It was then that I began to think I wanted to go home.

I was twenty-eight years old in 1947–48, and while I was not exactly overwhelmed with masculine attention, I was not exactly a wallflower either.

While I could sympathize with Dorrie, matrimony and the rigors of raising a family had little appeal for me even then. When the subject came up, I used to laugh and say I had sand in my shoes and did not want to settle down until I had a chance to see more of the world than I had seen so far. True, I had been back and forth across the country several times since I joined the Navy, but wartime billboards that one can still see occasionally had Uncle Sam pointing a finger and saying "Join the Navy (or the Army) and See the World!" His message was not "Join the Navy (or the Army) and see the United States," and sometimes I still feel like the war happened and I didn't get to go.

As the discharge and departure of our paralytic and badly handicapped patients to a veterans hospital or their home accelerated, and more and more of the medical staff began leaving the service that spring, rumors began circulating that the Corona Naval Hospital would be closed, and I grew more and more restless and was glad enough when orders arrived detaching me from duty at the Corona Naval Hospital and sending me closer to home:

> . . . effective on or about 11 May 1948 to arrive 8 June 1948 at the Great Lakes Naval Hospital for duty as physio-therapist.

Leave time spelled out was ample and welcome, but immediately I had another problem. What to do about my car? I had become quite attached to my car, and nobody I knew was heading east. Chicago was not all that attractive a destination for anyone who might take leave and travel with me. Since there seemed no solution to my problem, I went to the local Dodge dealer, had the Dodge checked out and prepared for a long trip, packed my gear in the trunk, and announced to friends and family that I had decided to go alone. And go I did, of course, but not as the crow flies. I took the long route north along the California coast, paused briefly in Santa Barbara, and didn't start my long trip east until I had seen the spectacular view of San Francisco from the top of the Mark (the Mark Hopkins Hotel, a much-touted gathering spot for military personnel during WWII), and driven across the Golden Gate Bridge.

The rest of the trip was sometimes interesting, sometimes boring, and always tiring. The ups, downs, and frequent curves driving through the mountains left little opportunity to relax and enjoy the scenery, unless I behaved like a tourist and stopped frequently to look around, and I was content coming down on the other side until I reached the desert and salt flats en route to Salt Lake City. Driving through the Great Salt Desert was not fun. The glare of the sun on the stark, white sand and salt without a tree or shrub to break the monotony, or even another traveler on the road, was both terribly hypnotic and a little frightening. When I finally caught a glimpse of the Great Salt Lake shimmering in the distance, I thought at first it was a mirage. (I learned later that one travels that road at night for cause. Air conditioning for cars had not yet been invented.)

I did not linger long in Salt Lake City. My lust for travel and adventure had cooled considerably since leaving San Francisco, and after a lonely ride across Wyoming, all I wanted was to arrive some place, any place where I did not have to rise and face another whole day on the road. But I was still many miles from Chicago and home, and there wasn't a whole lot of choice but to keep on driving until I got there.

Eventually I did get there, of course, but one incident that occurred along the road deserves to be mentioned and describes how things have changed since World War II. I was somewhere along the road in Wyoming or Nebraska, I'm not sure exactly where, but I was terribly road-weary, and the road seemed to go on and on with nothing ahead or behind me to break the monotony. On a long stretch of road, after an unintended nap at the wheel, I was startled awake and found myself driving on the wrong side of the road and heading for a deep ditch. Fortunately, there was no traffic heading west that morning, and I was able to get my car back on the right side of the road and under control without incident. It was another lesson learned, and I stopped early that afternoon to rest. Next day, however, I was still tired and wondering when I got back on the highway what I could do to help me stay awake. Just ahead I saw a hitchhiker, a no-no for a woman traveling alone, but I stopped anyway. I knew I needed someone to talk to, I needed someone to help me stay awake. My hitchhiker turned out to be a sailor on his way to some place in Indiana. He wasn't exactly in uniform, but he was carrying a duffel bag and wearing a dark jacket that could pass for a peajacket. He didn't talk much, but he did offer to help drive if I would drive on through to Chicago that same day. That was a no-no too, and this I declined even though I was neither worried nor afraid. When I announced that I was going to stop for the night, he merely asked that I let him out at a likely spot where he might more quickly get another ride.

Would I do such a thing as pick up a lonely traveler on an empty country road these days? Even if he was in uniform? Even if I was in familiar territory and not alone? No, I would not, but 1948 was different.

It was good to finally get home and to see my father and mother again. The war was over there too, with everybody busy getting on with their lives. My mother's wartime banner, with its stars for her children in the service, had been taken down and put away. I was the only one of her children still in uniform, and I think she hoped I, too, would soon be coming home to work in the local hospital. But unlike my brothers who had come home to Illinois to resume their prewar lives and occupations, I still wanted to see more of the world than I had seen during the war. Like the lilting lyric in an old song about the war years, "How do you keep them down on the farm after they've seem Par-e-e?"I hadn't yet seen Paris. Neither had I seen London, or Hawaii, or any other offshore lands, and I still wanted to see more of the world than the United States of America. A tour of duty at the Great Lakes Naval Hospital was unlikely to change that, of course, but a career in the Navy seemed to give me better odds that I might and had greater appeal for me as well.

U.S. Naval Hospital Great Lakes:
8 June 1948–5 July 1950

On June 8, 1948, I reported as ordered, ". . . to the Medical Officer in Command at Great Lakes Naval Hospital . . . ." I checked in with the chief nurse, got my room assignment in the nurses' quarters, unpacked and parked my car, and breathed a sigh of relief. After my long and lonely trek across country and the nearly ten days of sitting around doing nothing at home but listening to what everybody else at home from the war was doing, I was more than a little eager to get back to work. After registering my car and getting the necessary tag and permit for an assigned parking space, I headed for my new home away from home in the Great Lakes Naval Hospital nurses' quarters.

The nurses' quarters at Great Lakes had not changed much in five years, but the occupants had. Space now apparently was plentiful, and I had a private room for the first time in my Navy career. I thought at first I would like this, and I did for a while, but I missed the camaraderie I had grown used to, first with Fran as a student nurse at The Presbyterian Hospital School of Nursing, then with Ann, followed by Barbara at Great Lakes, Lois at Glenview and St. Albans, Josie in Richmond, and finally with Dorrie in Corona. Now several WAVE officers plus two or three Red Cross workers shared the nurses' quarters. Most of us had private rooms, but the camaraderie among the nurses that

I remembered and enjoyed during my first tour of duty at Great Lakes was missing. Everybody now seemed a bit restless, even a little bored, and I wondered if it might be my own restlessness that was to blame. Maybe, I thought, when I get back to work things will look a little better, but they never really did.

First stop next day, after reporting in duty uniform to be formally welcomed aboard by the chief medical officer, was to find my now official duty station, the hospital's Physical Therapy Department. It was not too difficult to find, but it was a bit difficult to be thrilled about it when I did. My new working environment was located in the basement of the dependents hospital. Compliments of a diligent corpsman, the place was neat and orderly, but the only daylight to be had came through dormer-type windows, basement-style, which were usually kept closed to keep out street noises. There was a fine view, if one cared to look out, of everybody's legs who might happen to be passing by.

The department's double doors opened on a well-furnished waiting room, without a single patient waiting there, a desk and chair, a telephone, an ancient typewriter, a small file room behind the desk with a couple of chairs and a small table on which an already percolating electric coffee pot was on hand to welcome me aboard. The treatment area was a long, ward-like room well supplied with treatment tables (waist-high, long, narrow tables, which were usually called plinths), a hubbard tank with tray and overhead lift used for debilitated patients getting underwater exercise (there was no other pool in the department), and various other heat and exercise equipment. It was already nine o'clock, and there was only one patient in the entire patient treatment area. He was stretched out on a treatment table getting a diathermy treatment to treat a stiff neck and back.

Things eventually got busier and a little better, of course, but the challenges I knew in Corona were missing. I liked the few patients who came to the department, the corpsman assigned to us, and Georgia, another Navy nurse subsequently trained as a physical therapist in Richmond and assigned to Great Lakes at her request after her apprenticeship program. What I found missing on my job at Great Lakes was the special challenge I had always felt working with paraplegic patients in Corona. Now I had what one might logically call a desk job, and I found the new freedom to run a Physical Therapy Department pretty much as I deemed appropriate was neither interesting nor rewarding. The war was now finally over for me too, and I missed having something more interesting and challenging to do than write reports that might never be read and count patients, treatments, and supplies.

Eventually I became friendly with Geri, a fine nurse who was wrestling with her own restlessness and not just a few unsolved problems of her own, with Susan who was a career WAVE officer worrying about her perceived obligation to go home to be with her aging mother, and the Red Cross workers who were there to clear out the Red Cross storage bin supplies and handle a few of the still lingering patient/family problems. I still have some of the handmade, old-fashioned Christmas tree ornaments the Red Cross workers gave me, which I still use on our Christmas tree each year, and an all-wool, knitted afghan left behind and never used when they cleared out their Red Cross storage bins on the base. I still cherish that old afghan these many years later, and I think of it as my good-luck blanket because I know it was made during the war for some sick or lonely soldier or sailor by an unknown, caring church or women's club lady. I always feel warmed by the love and care that must have gone into all those knit and purl stitches when I take it out of mothballs to use when it gets cold and drizzly outside and I feel chilled and lonely.

During the winter and early spring of 1949, my job had become increasingly dull, and Geri and I teamed up with two other nurses taking evening courses at the Lake Forest College, a two-year junior college program in Lake Forest, Illinois, a Chicago suburb easily reached by car. I wasn't particularly interested in acquiring additional college credit at that level because I had already graduated from a similar two-year college program in LaSalle, Illinois, before going on into nursing school. I decided, however, to register at the Lake Forest College and subsequently attended two semesters there, taking an evening course in beginning Spanish and a course called Contemporary Literacy. I also joined the women officers bowling team on the base that winter and went on to parties at the Officers Club where I met and dated a Marine lieutenant who made life in the peacetime Navy somewhat brighter and a lot more interesting for a while.

On 3 May 1949 I made full lieutenant, but my job was still dull and my romance with the Marine lieutenant was going nowhere. I took a short leave and a long trip back to Los Angeles that summer, but the Corona Naval Hospital was closing. Dr. Rod and even the rector of the little Episcopal church in Corona I had attended were gone, and I spent my leave going to the racetrack with a friend of the family in Los Angeles. I was very discouraged and glad enough to ride back to Chicago with my sister Ione's mother-in-law and her sick husband on the train.

Not much had changed while I was on leave, either on my job or with the Marine lieutenant I had been dating, and I was much relieved when one of the young doctors on the base came by and suggested we work with some of his patients on the wards who were bedfast and, for whatever reason, unable to come to the Physical Therapy Department for treatment. Suddenly things began to look interesting again. Exercise therapy for the seriously ill, exercise therapy

69

for bedfast patients who often are lonely and sometimes depressed. Here was the challenge for me I needed and the challenge I had been missing so badly.

One patient, whose name I have long since forgotten but whom I remember well, was an ancient sea captain, a retired Naval officer who looked a little like Santa Claus with a bushy, white beard and twinkling blue eyes. He was retired, in his late eighties, and in one of the private rooms in the main hospital building recovering from a mild heart attack. Orders for his treatment called for ". . . passive motion exercises to improve muscle tone, stimulate and increase muscular activity, and help get the patient up and about preparing him for discharge to his home." Remembering my experience working with "John Doe," the stroke patient I worked with in Corona, I decided to take this unusual assignment myself rather than pass it on to Georgia.

My first day working with the old captain went by with him lying quietly while I explained what I was going to do and then without comment letting me move his arms and legs through the range of motion. The next day he still said nothing as he lay there looking up at me while I took him through his passive exercise program. Finally, as I was preparing to leave, he looked up at me and said, "Lieutenant, why are we doing this? I'm an old man. I'm tired. Why don't you just pull up that chair and talk to me. Just talk to me. That's what I need. Tell me about yourself. I know what you are trying to do, but all this exercise business is my daughter's idea. I have lived my life, and I would get back on my feet a lot quicker if you would just sit down and talk to me awhile instead of pushing me into exercises that won't make me young again no matter what you do."

I didn't know what to say or do at first. Then I realized the old captain was serious, and I laughed. Soon we were both laughing, and I promised I'd come back next day and everyday while he was there for his exercise program if he would tell me sea stories about his life aboard ship. He had already mentioned he was skipper aboard the last sailing battleship before it was decommissioned after World War I. I have no idea whether it was true, but it didn't really matter. He was right, he needed to talk about his life at sea more than he needed an exercise program, and we both enjoyed a daily chat while I managed to get him doing a few passive bed exercises as well.

Perhaps the chat with the old sea captain I remember best after all these years was one shortly before his daughter came to take him home. He looked up at me and said, "Lieutenant, how come you aren't married yet?"

Without thinking, I grinned and replied, "I guess I just haven't met anybody lately who really wants to marry me, Captain."

Then I realized he wasn't joking, that he was concerned, and wanted to know why I often seemed discontented. That startled me enough to make me wonder if my discontent was that obvious to everybody I worked with. It also brought to mind a time when I was still a student nurse and the nursing school supervisor invited me to the linen room closet for a quiet chat about my attitude: "Was I happy? Unhappy? Did I really like nursing? Did I get along with the patients?" etc. It seemed a patient had complained to the head nurse on the floor about me, that I never smiled or acted like I cared about the patients or their problems. Obviously, I did survive the linen room chat with the student nurse supervisor, but I have never forgotten it, and I vowed anew that day to mend my ways.

The next day my chat-session with the old captain led to a discussion about the captain's daughters, who were both married to high-ranking Navy officers. I asked how they could possibly be that lucky to both find a high-ranking officer in the Navy who wasn't already married or who was just not the marrying kind. The old captain looked surprised,

71

chuckled softly, and said, "Women marry the men they meet, Lieutenant." We both laughed, but I knew the old captain was subtly telling me something he thought I should think about other than the obvious. His daughter came for him soon after that to take him home, and I did think about what he had been trying to tell me until I met Stony, another bedfast patient, a few days later.

Stony was a dedicated "fly-guy," a Navy pilot who survived the war in the Pacific and would willingly do it all over again given the opportunity if he could fly again. Stony had been grounded when he became critically ill with an infectious disease called Bacterial Endocarditis, a bacterial infection that attacks the heart valves and a disease which, at the time, was one from which few patients recovered. He was housed in an adjoining private room on one of the wards with orders for complete bed rest, no visitors except immediate family, and a liquid-to-soft diet as tolerated, meaning of course nothing by mouth to eat, but only things any healthy young flyer would never willingly put in his mouth unless he was starving.

The young doctor caring for Stony, sensing that his patient was suffering almost as much from inactivity and boredom as he was from his disease, came to Physical Therapy to ask if there was someone who could come to the ward and give Stony some light or passive bed exercises to help relieve the stress and boredom of prolonged inactivity. This was another assignment for me, and I suggested it might be better if he (the doctor) were to accompany me on the first visit so that the patient need not be alarmed. The doctor agreed it might be a good idea, and added with a laugh that he very much doubted the patient would be the least bit alarmed. "The guy refuses to believe he is sick, Lieutenant. He wants to get up and get back to the ship before they transfer him permanently to a desk job, and we just can't allow him to try that." He paused then went on. "Even if we were to let him up and around here too soon, he would probably get a nonstop poker game going with some of the guys on the ward, and that just might kill him. I wouldn't bet money on that either though. If any patient can get well with what that hotshot pilot has wrong with him, he is just the guy who might do it." That was Stony, and the doctor was right.

I spent a great deal of time with Stony that spring and summer. It was good for him as well as for me. Mostly we talked about flying. He talked. I listened. I had read his medical record and knew he was married. I also knew that his wife, who lived in Iowa with her mother and their two children, didn't often come to see him. He frequently talked about her, and I wondered why she did not come. She had to know he was seriously ill. Certainly the doctor would have told her, and the Red Cross would help if there was a family problem. I thought about asking Stony about this, but I decided after a while not to ask questions unless or until the subject came up, and it never did.

Later that spring Stony was finally allowed up and around on the ward, with results much as the doctor had predicted. Next he was allowed to get out and around on the base, if accompanied by a corpsman. I no longer went to the ward. Instead he came to the Physical Therapy Department for his exercise program, which usually became only a cup of coffee and a visit with anyone who happened to be available. I cared a lot about Stony, and when the doctor finally gave him a thumbs-up permission for liberty off the base as long as he had someone with him who understood his health situation, I was delighted to oblige. I knew of a nice restaurant in Waukegan, a town close by, and we went out for dinner there. That again was good for him as well as for me, and we went out quite often after that, always with a fold-up, lightweight wheelchair available in the trunk of my car in case he got over-tired and needed assistance getting back to the base.

Stony soon was getting well enough to go home on sick leave. I knew this and was glad for him, but when the time came for him to go and I took him to the train, I knew what the old captain had been trying to tell me. My little world once again became grim and dreadfully boring. I was missing Stony too much, and I began wondering what to do about my life without someone or at least something more stable to care deeply about.

In the summer of 1949 I was thirty years old. Most of my close friends were married and raising a family, and I still did not know what I really wanted to do. Did I really want a career? Should I stay in the Navy? Certainly peace-time Navy had not been a very rewarding experience so far, and I asked myself what I ought to be doing about it. Should I resign, and if I resigned, where could I go? Where could I find a job that would allow me to travel, a job that would provide a challenge like the one I had had in Corona? At a veterans hospital? Maybe, but I had no answer for any of these questions, and I finally decided the thing to do was to go back to school to get a graduate degree either in Nursing or Physical Therapy via the GI Bill. After that, I probably would be able to decide what to do next.

Meanwhile, I was worrying about Stony. Was he all right? Was he glad to get home? Was his wife glad to see him? I still wondered why she had failed to visit him all those months when he was so ill. Didn't she care about him? He had never really discussed his marriage with me, and I knew that I had begun to care too much for this Navy pilot now turned patient, and that I was jealous of his wife.

With Stony away on sick leave, Geri transferred, and Susan off on a cruise with her mother, I felt left behind, bored, and terribly discontented. At about the same time my attention was diverted by a rumor that the chief medical officer had decided it would be a nice gesture to have a beauty salon installed in the dependents hospital. He had also decided, ". . . what better place to install it than in the basement of the dependents hospital?" I thought it was a good idea, too, until I learned the exact location he had in mind was in one end of the Physical Therapy Department that we seldom used now and no longer really needed based on our declining patient count. I did wonder, however, how all that would come down relative to the setup in my department.

I was soon to find out when the "skipper" (the chief medical officer), the executive officer, and the chief nurse marched into the department unannounced and started making plans for the proposed layout for the beauty salon. The waiting room for the Physical Therapy Department would remain unchanged. They decided there was plenty of room and even adequate furniture there. My desk and phone would serve nicely, with no need for an additional phone line for the beauty salon. At this point in the planning there was cause for alarm. Was it to be my new responsibility to function as receptionist for the new beauty salon? I had the temerity to ask, to question that particular part of the plan, and the skipper and crew paused only long enough for him to let me know I had erred in questioning his plans for my future activities before he turned abruptly and they all stalked out.

The next day I was invited to report to the chief nurse's office to be told that the skipper had asked for my fitness report for the purpose of changing it to indicate I was uncooperative. She said she was sorry about what had happened, and that she felt she should warn me that I would be expected to sign the revised fitness report without challenge. Naturally, I was shocked at first. Then I was angry. When I said nothing, she went on to explain that it had been wrong for me to question the captain's authority, and told me not to worry too much about it, that it was only a small change and probably wouldn't really matter much in my future career in the Navy.

But it did matter, and I asked myself an important question. Did I really want to work in an environment where an "Aye, aye, sir" was obligatory to get along, whether I agreed with a senior officer's dumb idea or not? The answer was no, and I decided the time had come for me to do some serious thinking about my future. The war now really was finally over for me. Like Stony, I did not want to spend my life "flying" a desk in between wars, and I certainly had no wish to be a receptionist in a beauty salon. I wrote and sent the following letter dated 27 March 1950 asking for a leave of absence to go back to school:

```
To: Chief of Naval Personnel, Navy Department,
Washington DC
Via: (1) Commanding Officer (2) Chief, Bureau
of Medicine and Surgery
Subj.: Leave of absence; request for

1. It is requested that I be granted a leave
of absence from duty in the Nurse Corps, US
Navy, for the period of one year, this period
to begin on or about 1 July 1950.

2. This request is made because:

    a. In three years of work in Physical
    Therapy I have had a growing interest
    in the field of Rehabilitation, and I am
    anxious to spend some time in research
    in that field.
```

b. I need two semesters of academic work on the campus to complete work toward a Bachelor of Science degree.

c. I feel that I am capable in a teaching situation and with the proposed work in Rehabilitation plus a degree in Nursing Education I shall be in a position to do the work in which I am most interested and one for which I believe there is a pertinent need.

3. This request is made without request for nor expectation of Navy support or remuneration.

4. In the event that granting leave of absence is not in accord with existing policy of the Nurse Corps, it is requested that this letter be considered as resignation from the Nurse Corps, U.S. Navy, and that I be placed on inactive reserve status on or about the aforementioned date.

Did I write all this without help? I wish I could say that I did, but it just was not so. I had help, help from the hospital personnel officer, who proved both a good friend and a fine counselor in advising me to leave the door open, that I might change my mind or that I might want to come back after I finished my education. At the time I could not imagine that either situation might occur, but they did.

Response from the Chief of Naval Personnel to my request for a leave of absence dated 11 April 1950 arrived and was delivered to me as follows by the hospital personnel office:

Via: Commanding Officer, U.S. Naval Hospital, Great Lakes, Illinois as "FIRST ENDORSEMENT" on 17 April 1950.
Subj.: Extended leave of absence.
Ref.: (a) Your ltr NH 13(17)/304393W . . . of 27 Mar 1950

1. The receipt of reference (a) is hereby acknowledged.

2. Your request for one year's leave of absence for the purpose of attending school and doing research work in the field cannot be complied with as it is not the practice to grant such extended leave of absence.

3. If you still desire to return to school, your resignation should be submitted in accordance with Article C-10336, Bureau of Naval Personnel.

Now I had to decide. Do I quit a good job without deciding what to do next? I admit to second thoughts then, and several times later after Stony came back from leave early looking very tired and ill. He had only been home a few days before taking off to see an old flying buddy. They had gone flying, got together with some of the fellows, had a few drinks, and he decided he did not want to go home. Instead he went to visit his parents and discovered he really was not well, that he needed to get back to the hospital, and that he had to accept that maybe his flying days really were over. I was sympathetic, of course, and I decided then that I, too, must accept that it was time for me to get on with my life.

The decision to resign was not easy for me. Neither was it entirely uncomplicated. On 8 May 1950 a letter signed by the Assistant Secretary of the Navy, addressed to me with multiple copies covering every facet of life in the service, arrived:

```
Via: Commanding Officer
Subj: Acceptance of Resignation from the
      U.S. Navy
Ref:  (a) Your resignation dated
          17 April 1950
      (b) BUPers CL 207-49

Encl: (1) Application Form
```

1. When directed by your commanding officer on or about 1 July 1950 you will regard yourself detached from all duties which may have been assigned you. In accordance with reference (b), you will report immediately to your commanding officer for temporary duty in connection with your separation processing.

2. Upon completion of separation processing, and when directed by the commanding officer of the activity at which you are separated, you will regard yourself detached. By direction of the President, your resignation from the U.S. Navy is accepted under honorable conditions to take effect at 2400 on the date of detachment from such activity.

3. Upon final detachment, furnish the Bureau of Naval Personnel (attention Pers-3126) one copy and the disbursing officer carrying your

pay accounts four copies of these orders
bearing all endorsements.

4. Please acknowledge receipt of these
orders and inform the Bureau of Naval
Personnel of your permanent home address
upon detachment.

5. Disbursing officers will charge cost of
all travel to the appropriation in effect
on date of initial detachment, as follows:
To appropriation 1701454, TRNP 1950,
Expenditure Account 74110, when detachment
occurs in fiscal year 1950, in accordance with
section 605, Public Law 434, 81st Congress;
to appropriation Military Personnel, Navy,
when detachment occurs in fiscal year 1951.

Did I know and understand what all the directions in item
5 were about? Of course I did not, but I did know it referred
to my payroll account and that I was really out of a job and
a place to live as soon as all these data were collected. But
there was still another decision I had to make.

A letter from the Chief of Naval Personnel, dated 11 May
1950 addressed to me, Via Commanding Officer, Naval Hospital, Great Lakes, Ill. informed me as follows:

Subj.: Appointment in the Naval Reserve:
information concerning:

1. The Navy Department desires to bring to
your attention the opportunity which exists,
upon separation from the Regular Navy, to
continue your association with the Naval
Reserve with the rank and date of rank of

your last appointment in the Regular Navy,
providing you apply for appointment within
one year of the date of your release from
the Regular Navy, and are accepted by an
administrative board of review.

2. It is assumed that you would want to
return to active duty in the Naval Service
in time of war or national emergency. An
application form and franked envelope are
enclosed for your convenience. Upon receipt
of the completed form, the Chief of Naval
Personnel will initiate the action necessary
to effect your appointment.

An item 3. went on to describe what all this might mean
relative to what might be expected, and for purposes here
can be summed up as follows: Service in the Naval Reserve
counts as service for purposes of longevity pay in the event
the officer should be ordered to active duty. They (the Naval Reserve) are required to serve on active duty in time of
war or national emergency when so ordered by the Navy
Department.

Since this letter seemed to give me time to change my
mind about a Navy career, I took leave for eight days, beginning 13 May and returning 21 May 1950, to think about
what I ought to do next. I took my leave but reached no
firm decision by 21 May, so I decided to do nothing about
joining the Naval Reserve until I tried my luck at becoming
a civilian again.

On 5 June 1950, however, as ordered I reported to the
personnel officer to swear to and sign some discharge papers. Among them was the application for transfer to the
Naval Reserve. The personnel officer, when asked if I needed
to join the USNR before being detached, laughed and assured

me that it was not only not necessary but was also not advisable if I was planning to go back to school. "The Korean conflict is just beginning to heat up, Lieutenant," he went on, "and you might not make it through the gate before you are called back to duty." Thus, in essence, the last decision was made for me. On July 5, 1950, I packed my gear and drove my little old Dodge through the gate at the Great Lakes Naval Hospital without looking back.

Epilogue

World War II was over. I did not know it then, but my personal war was just beginning. That, however, is a whole different story and one common enough among veterans. Settling down to begin an old way of life right where you left off six or seven years earlier can be a daunting experience, particularly for those veterans who know and sometimes still dream about what it was like to have someone trying to kill them. No one was shooting at me during World War II, but caring for those who did and who survived the shooting and horrors of the war was the high point in my nursing career.

Did I ever get to see some of the other someplace(s) else that I wanted so badly to see? Yes, I did. I vacationed in Mexico in 1952; went back to Mexico in 1953 to attend summer school at the University of Mexico in Mexico City; spent a week in Cuba in 1955; two weeks in Spain in 1958 with side trips to Gibraltar and Tangiers; spent several weeks in Lima, Peru, in 1960 with side trips to Machu Picchu and Cuzco; spent several two-week vacations in Puerto Rico, Tortola, and the Virgin Islands. I met my husband at a ballroom dance contest in San Juan, Puerto Rico, in 1968. We were married in New York City in December 1970.

Photographs

Graduation Class of 1942 Presbyterian Hospital School of Nursing

NURSE WITH NAVY
NOW AS AN ENSIGN

Ensign Elizabeth E. Kinzer

Miss Elizabeth E. Kinzer, daughter of Mr. and Mrs. E. R. Kinzer of North of Utica , has been called to active service with The United States Navy as a nurse and is now Stationed at Great Lakes, Ill. With the rank of Ensign.

Ensign Kinzer is a graduate of the Sion School north of Utica, Ottawa Township High School in 1937, and LaSalle-Peru-Oglesby Junior College in 1939. In October, 1939, she entered Presbyterian Hospital School Of Nursing in Chicago , graduating from there in October, 1942. She enlisted in the Navy in May and was called into active service Aug. 31.

Ensign Kinzer is the third child of Mr. and Mrs. E.R. Kinzer to enter the service and the 14th grandchild of Mrs. Joseph Kinzer in the service. The other grandchildren are Capt. Richard Kinzer, stationed in Detroit, Mich., and Cpl. Ernest Kinzer of Ft. Sam Houston, Tex., sons of Mr. And Mrs. E.R Kinzer of north Utica; Capt. Harold Levy of the air corps, stationed in Florida, and Jean Levy o f the WAC stationed at Ft. Oglethorpe, Ga., children of Mr. And Mrs. Arthur Levy of Streator; T/Cpl. Howard Kinzer, in the army medical corp. and stationed in California, and Cpl. Arnold Kinzer, overseas, sons of Mr. And Mrs. Dean Kinzer; PFC Russell Kinzer Of Bowling Green, Ky., a son of Mr. And Mrs. Lawrence Kinzer of Utica township; Sgt. Cedric Kinzer, of Ft. Leonard Wood, Mo.; A/C Russell Kinzer, of Texas, and his Twin brother , Cpl. Robert Kinzer of Ft. Riley, Kas. , sons of Mr. And Mrs. Rolland Kinzer Of Valley City, N.D.; Sgt. Guy Kinzer of the marines, in the South Pacific; Sgt. Dean Kinzer of the marines in the personnel department in San Diego, Calif. recovering from shrapnel wounds in both legs suffered in action at Guadalcanal, and Cecil Kinzer, Navy, stationed at Great Lakes, sons of Mr. And Mrs. Ward Kinzer of Chicago.

The Daily Times, Ottawa, Illinois, July 1943

A short trip across the border

ELIZABETH KINZER WINS LIEUTENANCY

UTICA -- The navy needs more nurses like Elizabeth Emma Kinzer, daughter of Mr. and Mrs. Ernest R. Kinzer, Rt. 1, Utica, who has recently been promoted. Now her title is Lt. (jg) Elizabeth E. Kinzer, (NC), USNR.

Navy Nurse Kinzer was born Aug. 3, 1919 in Utica, attended Ottawa Township High School, La Salle-Peru-Oglesby Junior College for two years, and Presbyterian Hospital School of Nursing where she received the RN degree. She entered the U. S. Navy Reserve July 6, 1943 in Chicago with title of Ensign. Her first tour of Navy duty was at the U. S. Naval Hospital, Great Lakes. She served there from September, 1943 to March, 1944, reporting on March 31 for duty at the US Naval Air Station, at Glenview, Illinois. She has been assigned to the medical dispensary there since that time. She resides at the air station bachelor officers' Quarters.

The Daily Times, Ottawa, Illinois, April 1945

Fly guys help us celebrate our promotion

We teach Basic Nursing Care to train enlisted personnel for sea duty

Roommate Lois and I in full dress uniform off to visit NYC as tourists

Navy nurses in duty uniform at St. Albans Naval Hospital

First class of Navy Nurses sent to Physical Therapy School

Splendid driveway to Main Building at Corona Naval Hospital

Physical Therapy staff and interns at Corona Naval Hospital in 1946

"Dr. Rod" with ward nurse "Cissy" and me on a paraplegic ward at Corona Naval Hospital

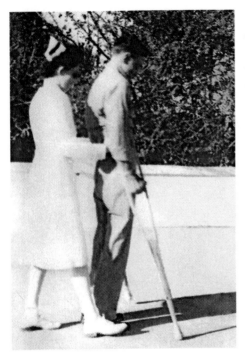

A paraplegic patient with low-back spinal cord injury ventures outside on crutches with physical therapy intern's assistance

"Frank" with low-back spinal cord injury ventures outside without assistance

Special patient "Pete" is learning to accept and adjust to his handicap

Special service for nursing staff at chapel on base in Corona is well attended

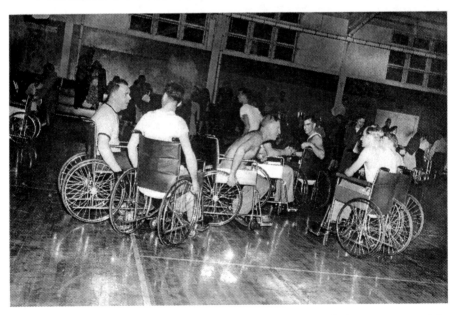

Wheelchair basketball team gets organized for game with doctors in wheelchairs

The Officers Club at Corona has charm as well as a boathouse and lake

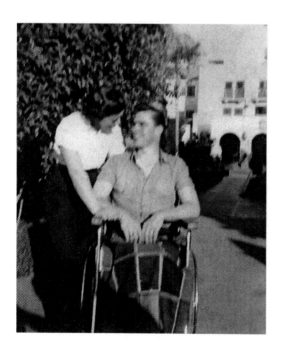

Encouragement works.
I'm proud of Pete's prog-
ress and tell him so

97

George is a bartender, a therapist, a friend if you need one, and a host to a gaggle of wild ducks and geese that come in off the lake for brunch

Okay, guys, line up. George is ready when you are

My Dodge and I make a long trip alone back east to Great Lakes in 1948

The troops gather for military honors and awards ceremony for retiring chief nurse

THE
PRESIDENT
OF
THE UNITED STATES OF AMERICA

To all who shall see these presents, greeting:

Know Ye, that reposing special trust and confidence in the patriotism, valor, fidelity and abilities of ELIZABETH E. KINZER, I do appoint her, by and with the advice and consent of the Senate, in the a Lieutenant of the Nurse Corps

United States Navy

to rank as such from the first day of January, nineteen hundred and forty-nine. This Officer will therefore carefully and diligently discharge the duties of the office to which appointed by doing and performing all manner of things thereunto belonging.

And I do strictly charge and require those Officers and other personnel of lesser rank to render such obedience as is due an officer of this grade and position. And this Officer is to observe and follow such orders and directions from time to time, as may be given by me, or the future President of the United States of America, or other Superior Officers acting in accordance with the laws of the United States of America.

This commission is to continue in force during the pleasure of the President of the United States of America, for the time being, under the provisions of those Public Laws relating to Officers of the Armed Forces of the United States of America and the component thereof in which this appointment is made.

Done at the City of Washington, this twenty-fourth day of August, in the year of our Lord one thousand nine hundred and forty-nine, and of the Independence of the United States of America the one hundred and seventy-fourth

By the President:

Registered

A. E. Parker
for the Chief of Naval Personnel.

Francis P. Matthews
Secretary of the Navy

Effective 1 January 1949

100

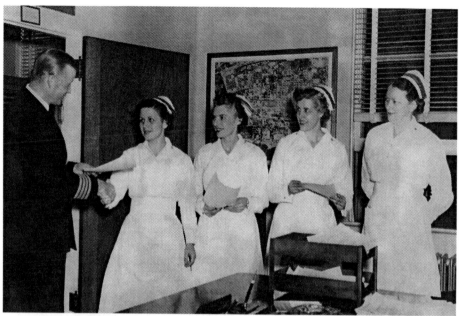

Full LOUIES now

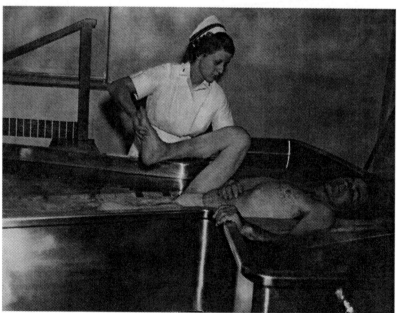

Hydrotherapy for exercise sometimes helps a stroke patient
at Great Lakes Naval Hospital

10023

from the Armed Forces of the United States of America

This is to certify that

Lieutenant Elizabeth E. Kinzer, NC, U.S.N. (304393)

was Honorably Discharged from the

United States Navy

on the 5th day of July, 1950. This certificate is awarded as a testimonial of Honest and Faithful Service

John F. Floberg

JOHN F. FLOBERG
Assistant Secretary of the Navy for Air

AUG 1 1950

Mom and Dad's "V for Victory Flag" with Stars

Captain Richard and
Corporal Ernest

Corporal Emile

Chaplain Bernard

Ensign Elizabeth

103

About the Author

Elizabeth Kinzer O'Farrell is a retired Nurse/Physical Therapist who lives with her husband in Tallahassee, Florida. She is a writer and member of the local chapter of the World War II Historical Society and the Tallahassee Writers' Association.

Usually called "Betty" by family and friends, Elizabeth grew up with six brothers, four of whom were also World War II veterans, and two sisters in a rural community ninety miles southwest of Chicago. She graduated from a local high school, LaSalle-Peru-Ogelsby Junior College in LaSalle, Illinois, and The Presbyterian Hospital School of Nursing in Chicago. After graduating from the School of Nursing in the fall of 1942, she joined the United States Navy Nurse Corps in 1943.

Elizabeth's first duty assignment was at the Great Lakes Naval Hospital in Waukegan, Illinois. In 1944 she was transferred from the Great Lakes Naval Hospital to the naval dispensary at the U.S. Naval Air Station in Glenview, Illinois. There she says she began to see what war was all about and what it meant to the eager young men preparing to fly planes that would be taking off and landing on a ship in unfriendly seas.

In 1945 Elizabeth was transferred again, this time to the U.S. Navy Hospital in St. Albans, New York, where she first learned to care for badly disabled young men being flown in from hospital ships and overseas treatment centers to stateside naval hospitals nearest to their homes.

The war in Europe was winding down in 1946, and the Navy, preparing for the thousands of disabled veterans coming home from overseas treatment centers and hospital ships, assigned Elizabeth and fifteen other Navy nurses to the Baruch Center of Physical Medicine in Richmond, Virginia, for instruction and training as physical therapists to replace the many WAVE therapists who were leaving the service on the point system. The program at the Baruch Center was a six-month crash course followed immediately by a six-month internship at a naval hospital under the supervision of a physiatrist.

Elizabeth graduated from the Physical Therapy course at the Baruch Center and took her internship at the Corona Naval Hospital in California. She says of her duty there, both as intern and graduate physical therapist, that she never worked harder or enjoyed her work more than she did the eighteen months she worked with the paralytic patients at the Corona Naval Hospital.

In May 1948 she received orders to report for duty once again at the Great Lakes Naval Hospital, this time ". . . for duty as physio-therapist." Duty at Great Lakes proved not very challenging for Elizabeth, and she decided she needed to get on with her life. She resigned her commission in 1950 to go back to school, but going back to school didn't prove very challenging either. Neither did general-duty nursing, and Elizabeth, not unlike many other veterans, experimented in a variety of jobs that led her finally to a job reviewing and writing copy for textbook ads in a nursing journal published by the Medical Division of McGraw-Hill Book Company in New York City. She did go back to school but took evening courses at New York University in editing and magazine publishing. Eventually she became Managing Editor for the *Journal of Nursing Education* published by the Medical

Division of McGraw-Hill Book Company, and later as Editor for the *Journal of Nursing Administration* published by Contemporary Publishing, Inc. in Wakefield, Massachusetts.

In 1973 Elizabeth and her husband moved to Tucson, Arizona, where she did some freelance editing and writing for and/or with staff personnel in the College of Nursing at the Arizona State University.

During the twelve years she and her husband lived in Tucson, Elizabeth was an active member of The National League of American Pen Women, Inc. and an associate member of the Society of Southwestern Authors. She retired in 1984, and moved with her husband to Tallahassee later that year.

CyPress Publications

PO Box 2636
Tallahassee, FL, 32316-2636
Voice: (850) 576-8820
Fax: (850) 576-9968
lraymond@nettally.com
http://cypress-starpublications.com

To order copies of *WW II . . . A Navy Nurse Remembers* by mail, please photocopy this page, fill out the information below, and mail to the address above. Please include check or money order in the amount of $18.42 ($12.95 + $0.97 tax + $4.50 shipping and handling) made out to CyPress Publications.

Name _____

Address _____

Phone _____

E-mail _____

Thank You for Your Order!

Visit our website for ordering information and news of upcoming titles.
http://cypress-starpublications.com

LaVergne, TN USA
19 November 2010
205546LV00011B/119/A